CALLED TO BE A COMMUNICATING CHURCH

A NATIONAL PASTORAL PLAN FOR SOCIAL COMMUNICATIONS IN INDIA

To

Sr. Angela Ann Zukowsky

with

Appreciation, admiration & gratitude

for your

initiatives & commitment to communications

Henry D'Souza

New Delhi

25. 11. 04

CALLED TO BE A COMMUNICATING CHURCH

A NATIONAL PASTORAL PLAN FOR SOCIAL COMMUNICATIONS IN INDIA

Abp Oswald Gracias
Bp Antony Devotta
Bp Leo Cornelio

Edited By
Henry D'Souza

CBCI COMMISSION FOR SOCIAL COMMUNICATIONS

Media House
Delhi
2004

2004

CALLED TO BE
A COMMUNICATING CHURCH
A NATIONAL PASTORAL PLAN FOR SOCIAL COMMUNICATIONS IN INDIA

Edited By
Henry D'Souza

Cover Design: Joby Mathew

Published and Distributed by:

Media House, 375-A, Pocket 2, Mayur Vihar Phase - I, Delhi 110 091, India
Ph: 011-22750667, 22751317, Fax: 011-22757040
E-mail: mediabooks@hotmail.com / books@indiancurrents.com

Printed at:
Jyoti Printers, E-94, Sector - 6, Noida, U.P. India. Ph: 0120-2422117, 3950599

ISBN: 81-7495-192-X

FOREWORD

I am happy to declare that this book, "CALLED TO BE A COMMUNICATING CHURCH" is a fruit of the four-day long historic conference on communication held in the very comfortable surroundings of *Atma Darshan* in Mumbai. Present with us in the Conference were Chairmen Bishops of all the Regional Communications Commissions, the Executive Secretary of the FABC OSC, the Secretaries of all the Regional Commissions and Presidents and Secretaries of our Communication Associations – Signis India and ICPA, and many eminent journalists. In this sense the Conference was indeed a historic one, for we had a galaxy of eminent media personnel there.

During the first two days, the Bishops met first among themselves and then with the Secretaries of their Commissions. The first day, the Bishops received input from an eminent HRD specialist, Mr. Allywn Fernandes who exposed us to public relations and effective use of media opportunities. It was a unique and profitable experience with hands on training. The second day with the Secretaries was more of a business meeting, where we discussed the implementation of the Final Statement of the CBCI General Body Meeting 2004.

Our General Body Meeting in Trichur in January 2004 took Social Communications as its theme. Seeing the urgency, relevance and importance of this topic the Standing Committee decided to study this subject in depth. At the end of the Conference the CBCI General Body issued a Statement. The Statement was unique in the sense that it was not just a message but focused on the formation of a pastoral programme. It was the intention of the Bishops in the General Assembly to see how the Church could become a more communicating Church. The richness of the input and the discussions of the CBCI General Body Meeting are reflected in the Final Statement.

The media we know are a "gift from God". They are given to us for the service of humanity. By themselves they are neutral but their effects are not. According to their use and the motives of those who handle the media, their effects come out as positive or negative. The media can be used to manipulate people. They can also be used to educate, entertain and help all to grow so that we have a fuller life.

We know that the media scenario in India is changing tremendously. Spectacular progress has been made in the field, particularly in electronic communication. This is making a profound influence on the lives of children and youth who are the future of tomorrow. Those of us who are very much involved in the media are very conscious of this. The Church cannot be a silent spectator to these developments, but given its thrust for the service of all people, it has a duty to make its contribution in this field as well. The Church seeks to give adequate pastoral care both to media persons and media users. All this was discussed at depth at the Trichur Meeting.

This Conference is but the first step in the implementation of the Final Statement of the CBCI. The CBCI had made two specific recommendations with regard to the follow up. The first step asked for an evaluation of all the communication centres in the country. This evaluation is meant to assess, prioritise and see what area needs to be strengthened. For this purpose an instrument in the form of a set of questionnaires has been prepared.

Secondly, the General Body asked that a National Pastoral Plan for Communications be prepared. It is the hope of the CBCI General Assembly that has a result of this meeting, every diocese would bc ablc to prepare its own pastoral plan for communications and integrate communications component into its pastoral plan. The final plan was presented to the CBCI Standing Committee for approval, so that it can be sent to the different dioceses for adaptation to the local needs according to the circumstances.

The National Conference was indeed a unique opportunity to discuss, plan and spearhead the communication apostolate in India. I consider it a special occasion to be able to give an impetus to the communications ministry in India. This book is a modest effort by the CBCI Commission for Social Communications in making the Church truly a communicating Church. Our desire is that communications media continue to be at the service of humanity and always used for the glory of God and spread of His Kingdom.

+ Oswald Gracias
Archbishop of Agra and
Chairman, CBCI Commission for Social Communications

India Communications Day
Sunday, Nov. 14, 2004

TABLE OF CONTENTS

Introduction

PART I

1. Called to be a Communicating Church - A National Pastoral Plan for Social Communications 01
2. Called to be a Communicating Church - the Final Statement of the CBCI General Body Meeting 2004 31

PART II

3. Called to be a Communicating Church - Some Reflections for Planning *by Fr Franz-Josef Eilers, svd* 39

4. Ways to Improve Professionalism in Catholic Publications
   4.1 How to Improve Professionalism in Catholic Publications *by Fr M.A. Joe Antony, sj* 58
   4.2 Promoting Professionalism in Catholic Publications and Productions *by Fr Alphonse Elengikal, ssp* 66
   4.3 The Mission and Vision of a Church-run Secular Publication *by Fr Xavier Vadakkekara, ofm. cap* 71

5. Training in Communications
   5.1 Is the Church in India Media Savvy? *by Michael Gonsalves* 80
   5.2 An Action Plan to Sensitize Church Leaders *by Bp Leo Cornelio, svd* 85
   5.3 Training in Communication for Priests, Religious and those in Formation *by Bp Chacko Thottumarickal, svd* 90
   5.4 Professional Training for the Church and Mainstream Media *by Fr Sebasti L. Raj, sj* 96
   5.5 Training of Lay People in Communications *by K.M. Selvaraj* 101
   5.6 Leveraging Media Interaction into an Opportunity *by Allwyn Fernandes* 106

6. Improving Coordination, Networking and Accountability
6.1 Coordination of Communications Activities at Regional/ Diocesan Level *by Fr Cedric Prakash, sj* 112
6.2 Improving Coordination, Networking and Accountability *by Fr Dominic Emmanuel, svd* 117
6.3 Coordination of Communications Activities in Tamil Nadu *by Fr Vincent Chinnadurai* 121
6.4 Parish Communication Committee (PCC) *by Fr Arun Ignatius Abraham, sj* 126

7. Networking and News-Sharing
7.1 Networking and News Sharing Among Publications *by Fr George Veliparambil* 132
7.2 Sharing News *by Fr Francis D'Britto* 136

8. Distribution System for Media Productions and Publications
8.1 A Strategy for Distribution *by Sr Anne Plathara, dsp* 142
8.2 Distribution System of Media Productions *by Fr Darryl D'Souza, sdb* 146
8.3 A Distribution Mechanism *by Fr Dominic Emmanuel, svd* 151

9. Promoting Alternative Media
9.1 Mission and Alternative Media *by Fr Eugene* 156
9.2 Fostering Alternative Media for Proclamation *by Fr Denis D'Sa* 160
9.3 Street Theatre and the *Awaaz* Troupe *by Fr John Paul Herman, svd* 165

10. Addresses
10.1 CBCI Commission for Social Communications 170
10.2 Regional Commissions 171
10.3 Participants of the National Conference on Communications 175

INTRODUCTION

Pope John Paul II in his encyclical, *Redemptoris Missio,* declaring the profound importance of the modern means of communications says, "The first Areopagus of the modern age is the world of communications which is unifying humanity and turning it into what is known as a 'global village'". Strongly emphasising the universal importance of communications he continues, "The means of social communications have become so important as to be for many the chief means of information and education, of guidance and inspiration in their behaviour as individuals, families and within society at large." *(Redemptoris Missio, n. 37)*

Can the Church which plays such an important role in shaping the destiny of the world through its spiritual, educational and social apostolates, ever dare to be a silent onlooker of these dramatic changes? Far from suggesting that the "Church should stand aloof or try to isolate herself from the mainstream of these events", the Council Fathers saw the Church "as being in the very midst of human progress, sharing the experiences of the rest of humanity, seeking to understand them and to interpret them in the light of faith. It was for God's faithful people to make creative use of the new discoveries and technologies for the benefit of humanity and the fulfilment of God's plan for the world.... employing the full potential of the 'computer age' to serve the human and transcendent vocation of every person, and thus to give glory to the Father from whom all good things come". *(John Paul II, Message for the World Communications Day 1990)*

In recent years a lot more has been happening in India in the field of social communications. On the one hand unprecedented revolution has been gripping the country through telecommunications and Information Technologies. And on the other hand, the Church in India has been sensitising itself to benefit from this all pervading revolution and integrate it into the Church's life to foster a "new culture of communications in the Church". The culminating effort in this direction has been the CBCI General Body Meeting '04 deliberating of the theme, "Church and Social Communications" and coming out with a widely appreciated final statement, "Called to be a Communicating Church".

The biennial plenary of the Catholic Bishops' Conference of India, gave a clarion call to prepare a National Plan for Social Communications with "a vision and strategies to stimulate, inspire and promote Catholic activities in this field". It recognized that "Social Communications have a significant role to play in every aspect of the Church's mission" and urged that "they must be integrated into every Church ministry", so that "Pastoral Plan for Social Communications should become an integral part of the mission of the Church." *(CBCI GBM '04, n. 8)*

In responsc to thc above mandate, the Office of the CBCI Commission for Communications, in consultation with a few experts in the field, prepared a draft plan. It was circulated among the members of the CBCI Commission for Social Communications, Bishop Chairmen of the Regional Commissions and the Regional Secretaries of the Commissions. Finally, the draft was collectively scrutinized, discussed and passed by the National Conference on Social Communications which was held during Aug. 3 – 6, 2004 at *Atma Darshan*, Mumbai. Chairman of the CBCI Commission for Social Communications, Archbishop Oswald Gracias ably facilitated the process.

The final draft plan was presented to the CBCI Standing Committee, which met in Bangalore during September 15 – 17, 2004. It approved the National Pastoral Plan for Social Communications for implementation.

Through this Pastoral Plan, we are not making a fresh beginning. We are only streamlining and strategising what is being done with so much of dedication and hard work. In the words of the Pastoral Letter *Aetatis Novae*, we only express our "gratitude to those responsible for the creative communications work underway in the Church everywhere. Despite difficulties - arising from limited resources, from the obstacles sometimes placed in the way of the Church's access to media," and gratefully appreciate that "much has been, and continues to be, accomplished. The dedicated bishops, clergy, religious and lay people engaged in this critically important apostolate deserve the thanks of all." *(Aetatias Novae, n. 3)*

What has been done is good enough. But there is no scope either for dithering or for sitting back. The situation calls for a greater degree of urgency and deeper commitment. It calls for a concerted action and generation of synergy through united effort. In the words of the Vatican Document, "It is not only appropriate but 'necessary for Christians to work together more effectively in their communications efforts and to act in more direct cooperation with other religions to ensure a united religious presence in the very heart of mass communications." (*Criteria for Ecumenical and Inter-religious Cooperation in Communications*, n. 1).

Now the question is who has to implement this plan? Is it going to be one more plan, like many others of the past well prepared, widely promulgated and confined to the dust bin of time to gather dust? The Vatican Council II is clearly insisting on the urgency says, "All the members of the Church should make a concerted effort to ensure that the means of communication are put at the service of the multiple forms of the apostolate **without delay** and **as energetically as possible**." Then rightly so, the plan is in hand, the task is clear and the time to act is NOW.

In the name of CBCI Commission for Social Communications, I thank Abp Oswald Gracias for his meaningful foreword. A million thanks to all the Bishops and fellow communicators who have contributed to this publication. A word of gratitude to Brighty Sebastian and Arun Toppo for their dedicated secretarial support. A special thank to Media House for publishing this book.

Henry D'Souza
Executive Secretary
CBCI Commission for Social Communications

India Communications Day
Sunday, Nov. 14, 2004

PART I

1

CALLED TO BE A COMMUNICATING CHURCH

A NATIONAL PASTORAL PLAN FOR SOCIAL COMMUNICATIONS

A NATIONAL PASTORAL PLAN FOR SOCIAL COMMUNICATIONS

VISION-MISSION-ACTION

1. VISION

TO BUILD A COMMUNITY OF COMMUNITIES OF ALL PEOPLE IN THE SPIRIT OF JESUS CHRIST THROUGH SOCIAL COMMUNICATIONS.

2. MISSION

2.1 To proclaim the Good News through social communications.
2.2 To train Church personnel and laity in social communications.
2.3 To foster a culture of interactive communications at all levels.
2.4 To cultivate media/public relations.
2.5 To advance advocacy to uphold dignity and human rights of all, particularly the marginalized by creating public opinion.
2.6 To promote universal media education.
2.7 To publish/ produce people's need based programes.
2.8 To promote alternative media.
2.9 To celebrate Communications Day meaningfully.
2.10 To mobilize and allocate human and financial resources.
2.11 To promote accountability and transparency.

3. ACTION/ STRATEGIES

Strategy (Activity)	Responsibility
3.1 To proclaim the Good News through social communications:	
3.1.1 Rejuvenating diocesan Commissions and Communication Centres so that "they become truly institutions which communicate and network with local Christian media professionals and other like-minded persons, providing them with pastoral assistance." *(CBCI GBM '04, n. 7)*	3.1.1.1 Diocesan Bishop will constitute the commission. The commission will meet regularly to coordinate and supervise the ministry.
3.1.2 Motivating, animating and coordinating activities of the Catholic Media Organizations, communication institutes and communication Centres for optimum service to the community and society. *(YKJ National Assembly, 2000)*	3.1.2.1 National/regional/ diocesan commissions
3.1.3 Facilitating as soon as possible, in every region/diocese, setting-up of Commissions for social communications at the regional/diocesan levels, an office for social communications, and preparing a pastoral plans respectively.	3.1.3.1 Regional Chairmen/ Local Bishop/ Diocesan Pastoral Council/ Council of Priests.
3.1.4 Facilitating the identification and appointment of talented and trained spokespersons who can	3.1.4.1 Bishop/ Personnel Board

establish links at different levels – deanery/ diocesan/ regional/ national. *(CBCI GBM '04, n.12)*	
3.1.5 Keeping in place a Crisis Communication Team to manage crisis situations. Evolving an action plan to manage communications in the event of a crisis.	3.1.5.1 Bishop/Commission /Director
3.1.6 Identifying appropriate and talented church personnel and getting them trained for communications service.	3.1.6.1 Bishop/Commission /Director
3.1.7 Motivating church personnel and laity to communicate the Good News through their communication activities.	3.1.7.1 Director/ Council of Priests/ Pastoral Council
3.1.8 Motivating all church personnel to actively participate in the new opportunities created by media and the information technologies to share the Good News and spread the Kingdom of God by fighting the menace of crime, corruption and communalism. *(CBCI GBM '04, n. 4)*	3.1.8.1 Commission/Director/ Seminary Rector / Pastoral Centre
3.1.9 Acting as a watchdog on media issues.	3.1.9.1Commission/Director/ PRO
3.1.10 Assisting other church commissions in providing communications components in their respective services.	3.1.10.1 Commission/ Director

3.2 To train church personnel and laity in social communications:

3.2.1 To promote proper formation programmes to adequately train all leaders of the community, viz. bishops, priests, religious and lay, in communications so that they can effectively discharge their duties for evangelization and defence of the genuine interests of the church and society. *(CBCI GBM '04, n.17)*	3.2.1.1 National Commission/ regional commissions/ centres
3.2.2 To encourage adequate formation of seminary formators, future diocesan and religious priests to proclaim the Word effectively and celebrate the Sacred Mysteries meaningfully. Efforts must be made to improve their communication skills. A proper media course should be part of the seminary curriculum. *(CBCI GBM '04, n. 18)*	3.2.2.1 Bishop/Seminary Rector/ Dean of Studies
3.2.3 To facilitate the integration of communications training in to all formation - biblical, catechetical, educational, healthcare and other. *(CBCI GBM '04, n. 18)*	3.2.3.1 Pastoral Centre/ Catechetical Centre/Director
3.2.4 To make the catechists, teachers, leaders in parishes and religious institutions, social workers, and health personnel, living agents of communication to the public. *(CBCI GBM '04, n.19)*	3.2.4.1 Respective Commissions

3.2.5 Motivating the church personnel dealing with the publics to be people-friendly.	3.2.5.1 Respective Commissions
3.2.6 To identify and encourage creative young talented persons to pursue a career in the media, with a view to the future. *(CBCI GBM '04, n.19)*	3.2.6.1 Commission / Director
3.2.7 To facilitate starting of courses/ departments of communications in Catholic colleges and Institutes.	3.2.7.1 Commission / Director

3.3 To foster a culture of interactive communications at all levels:

3.3.1 Sensitising church personnel to promote a culture of communication through interaction, consultation, participation and collective action.	3.3.1.1 Director/ Commissions
3.3.2 Making the church periodicals, websites, news-letters, and notice-boards - channels of interactive communication.	3.3.2.1 Persons concerned
3.3.3 Training pastoral clergy, seminarians, religious and other church personnel in communication skills and media education.	3.3.3.1 Commission/ Director

3.3.4 Regularly upgrading the communication technology and equipment (telephone, e-mail etc) for better communication network in the diocese.	3.3.4.1 Bishop/Director/ PRO

3.4 To cultivate media/public relations:

3.4.1 Identifying, getting trained and appointing diocesan PRO.	3.4.1.1Bishop/Director
3.4.2 To uphold the legitimate rights of media, and network with the mainstream media to highlight people's concerns and the church's point of view. *(CBCI GBM '04, n.11)*	3.4.2.1 Commission/ Director
3.4.3 To cultivate good relations with media persons, invite them from time to time, for a friendly dialogue and fellowship. *(CBCI GBM '04, n.11)*	3.4.3.1 Commission/ Director
3.4.4 To give greater attention to the regional media, both print and electronic; to identify and train people for this work. *(CBCI GBM '04, n. 11)*	3.4.4.1 Commission/ Director
3.4.5 Instituting media awards for identifying and appreciating outstanding media persons.	3.4.5.1 Commission/Director

3.4.6 Organizing media seminars for sensitizing/ upgrading skills of media professionals.	3.4.6.1 Commission/Director
3.4.7 Defending the rights of media professionals in defence of the freedom of expression.	3.4.7.1 Commission/Director
3.4.8 Facilitating interaction with media persons, social activists and social thinkers to foster good will.	3.4.8.1 Commission/Director/ PRO

3.5 To advance advocacy to uphold dignity and human rights of all, particularly the marginalized by creating public opinion:

3.5.1 Working with the members of other churches and ecclesial communities, and with the followers of other religions, to "ensure a place for spiritual and moral values in the media." *(Ecclesia in Asia, n. 48)*	3.5.1.1 Commission/Director
3.5.2 Networking with media professionals of other faiths for relevant joint productions.	3.5.2.1 Commission/Director
3.5.3 Making human rights and human dignity content of media productions.	3.5.3.1 Commission/Director

3.5.4 Sensitising media professionals to human rights issues.	3.5.4.1 Commissions/Director
3.6 To promote universal media education:	
3.6.1 To encourage people to be media users and dutifully alert them to the threats being posed by the present mass media and educate them, particularly children and youth, to "use the media for authentic and wholesome lives in accordance with the plan of God." *(CBCI GBM '04, n. 4)*	3.6.1.1 Director / Diocesan Education Office
3.6.2 To impart media education, which is concerned with helping media, consumers develop an informed and critical understanding of the nature of the mass media, the techniques used by them, and the impact of these techniques. *(CBCI GBM' 04, n. 4)*	3.6.2.1 Commission/Director
3.6.3 To be concerned about the influence of media on the family and evolve programmes to make children, youth and parents appreciative, critical and discerning consumers of media. *(CBCI GBM '04)*	3.6.3.1 Relevant commissions / Director
3.6.4 Training of teachers and parents to impart media education.	3.6.4.1 Commission/Director

3.6.5 Organizing a Trainers Team to give media education.	3.6.5.1 Diocesan Director
3.6.6 Preparing resource material for media education for various sections such as children and youth.	3.6.6.1 Commission/Director
3.6.7 Networking with media advocacy groups and NGOs.	3.6.7.1 Commission/Director

3.7 To publish / produce people's need based programes:

3.7.1 Responding to issues concerning the community and responding to them effectively through write-ups, letters to the editor etc.	3.7.1.1 Commission/Director/ PRO
3.7.2 Managing communication during crisis situation with the help of Crisis Management Team.	3.7.2.1 Commission/Director/ PRO
3.7.3 Contributing articles and productions, and creating forums to build public opinion.	3.7.3.1 Commission/Director/ PRO
3.7.4 Producing programmes (songs, cassettes, radio / T.V and stage programmes) for proclamation, faith formation and social/human development	3.7.4.1 Commission/Director/ PRO

3.7.5 To improve the catholic periodicals, publications and media productions by bringing in more professionalism, in order to make them truly communicative. *(CBCI GBM '04)*	3.7.5.1 Commission/Director
3.7.6 Making available the productions done already and producing new ones as per need.	3.7.6.1 Commission/Director
3.7.7 Looking out for opportunities to participate in the local radio/ T.V./ Satellite Channels / Cable Networks.	3.7.7.1 Commission/Director
3.7.8 Whenever needed building infrastructure, such as audio /T.V studio, etc.	3.7.8.1 Bishop/ Commission/ Director
3.7.9 Encouraging local talents to participate in the local media facilities/ opportunities.	3.7.9.1 Commission/Director
3.7.10 Regularly improving and overhauling the mobile unit/ stage troupe for a better out-reach.	3.7.10.1 Commission/Director
3.7.11 Periodically conducting feedback/surveys to identify people's communication needs and to assessing the effectiveness of church's communication work.	3.7.11.1 Commission/Director

3.8 To promote alternative media:

3.8.1 To develop systematically, seriously and purposefully alternative media such as folk arts, dance, drama, music, *keertan*, *katha*, street-plays, Christmas cribs, Passion scenes etc. to reach out to the least and the last, of society. *(CBCI GBM '04)*	3.8.1.1 Commission/Director

3.9 To celebrate the Communications Day meaningfully:

3.9.1 To recognize that 'Communications Day' is a valuable opportunity to sensitize the community, celebrate the 'India Communications Day' with a meaningful liturgy and relevant programmes. The Holy Father's message for the day should be disseminated to the grassroots even beyond the Church through the secular media. *(CBCI GBM '04, n.18)*	3.9.1.1 Commission/Director

3.10 To allocate and mobilize human and financial resources:

3.10.1 Personnel: The Indian Church is abundantly blessed with talented and committed personnel among the clergy, religious and the laity.

Efforts should be made to identify them, adequately train them and appropriately utilize their services for the communications apostolate.	3.10.1.1 CBCI/ Commissions/ Bishops/ Major Superiors
3.10.2 Finances: The annual budget of the dioceses, institutions and organizations should "allocate means of obtaining and maintaining financial support adequate to the carrying-out of the pastoral plan." (*Aetatis Novae, n. 24*)	3.10.2.1 Bishops/Commissions / Heads of Institutions
3.10.3 "Requests the bishops and the faithful of India to allocate the Sunday collection of the India Communications Day for communications ministry as follows: diocesan communications commission: 40%, Regional Communications Commission: 30% and the CBCI Commission for Communications: 30%." *(CBCI SCM, New Delhi, 2002)*	3.10.3.1 CBCI/ Bishops/ Parishes
3.10.4 Communications Foundation: "Start a Communications Foundation with the Communication Day contributions and other donations and to utilize the proceeds of the fund to support communications ministry and prepare young talents for mainstream media." *(CBCI SCM, New Delhi, 2002)*	3.10.4.1 CBCI/ Commission/ Public

3.11 To promote accountability and transparency:

3.11.1 All official records and assets of the national/regional/diocesan Commissions/ centres and the Catholic Media Organisations should be maintained and handed over to the new incumbents while the new team of officers take over. Copies of the same may be sent to appropriate regional/national Commission Chairmen for information, continuity and transparency.	3.11.1.1 Respective Directors/ Secretaries/ Office Bearers
3.11.2 All the National Institutes, Commissions, Catholic Media Organizations and the Regional Commissions prepare an annual report of their respective activities and send it to the CBCI Commission Chairman by the end of August each year which would help in preparing a national consolidated report.	3.11.2.1 Secretaries/ Directors

4. Why a Pastoral Plan for Social Communications?

4.1 Communication is very basic to the very identity and mission of the Church

"Jesus Christ came to communicate the fullness of life so that all could have 'life, and have it in abundance (Jn. 10:10)'. The disciples of Jesus are commissioned to 'go and proclaim the good news to all nations' (Mt 28:19)." *(CBCI GBM '04, n. 6-7)*

4.2 Today's communications situation demands a planned approach

India too is experiencing a media explosion. The Indian society is profoundly influenced by the communication revolution. It is impacting all aspects of human life today. In such a situation, the Church in India cannot be a silent spectator. It needs to have a planned approach to communications apostolate.

4.3 The Church documents urge to have a Pastoral plan

Urging all the dioceses and Episcopal Conferences to have pastoral plans for communications the Vatican Document, Aetatis Novae says, "Catholic media work is not simply one more programme alongside all the rest of the Church's activities: social communications have a role to play in every aspect of the Church's mission. Thus, not only there should be a pastoral plan for communications, but communications should be an integral part of every pastoral plan, for it has something to contribute to virtually every other apostolate, ministry, and programme." *(AN, n. 17; also Inter Mirifica, n. 21; Communio et Progressio, n. 162, 165, 172; Redeptoris Missio, n. 37c)*

4.4 FABC OSC insists on a Pastoral Plan

"Every Bishops' Conference must have a Pastoral Plan for Communication, which includes also the communication dimension for every ministry of the conference. Such a Pastoral Plan is to incarnate the prophetic, proclaiming mission of the Church in media – shaped and media – conscious society." *(FABC BM '96)*

4.5 Request by the CBCI General Body Meeting 2004

"A Pastoral Plan for Social Communications should become an integral part of the mission of the Church. We request that the CBCI Commission for Social Communications to draw up a Pastoral Plan, which would include a vision and strategies to stimulate, inspire and promote Catholic activities in this field. Thereby, the whole apostolate of the media will be 'placed under a single, overall direction. *(Communio et Progressio*, n. 169)." *(CBCI GBM '04, n. 8)*

5. The Communications reality today

5.1 The emergence of a new media culture

The world is experiencing the emergence of a new culture that "originates not just from whatever content is eventually expressed, but from the very fact that there exist new ways of communicating, with new languages, new techniques and a new psychology". *(Redemptoris Missio, n. 37)*

5.2 The means of social communication have become chief means of information and education

"In an era of globalization, 'the means of social communication have become so important as to be for many the chief means of information and education, of guidance and inspiration in their behaviour as individuals, families and within society at large." *(Ecclesia in Asia, n. 48)*

5.3 The mass media are influencing universally

"Nowhere today are people untouched by the impact of media upon religious and moral attitudes, political and social systems, and education." *(Aetatis Novae, n. 1)*

5.4 The younger generation is growing in a media conditioned world

"In particular, the younger generation is growing up in a world conditioned by the mass media." (*Ecclesia in Asia*, n. 48)

5.5 Media are exercising profound influence in India

"India, we realize is making great strides in the field of Information Technology. The press, radio, cinema, television and other Information Technologies have expanded tremendously in the last few years. These have enabled people to relate and communicate to each other even when separated by long distances, thus building a world-wide-web. The media are exercising a great influence on the minds of the people and creating public opinion." *(CBCI GBM '04, n. 1)*

5.6 Media also have negative influences

"While the media bring information, education, and entertainment and create public opinion, they also have some negative influences. Some of the values propagated by the media are contrary to the Gospel and to our culture. An increase in violence can sometimes be traced to the influence of media. Family life, in particular, has been profoundly affected with the promotion of consumerism and values opposed to the sacredness of marriage being beamed into the home." *(CBCI GBM '04, n. 3)*

5.7 The Church's evangelizing mission too is deeply affected by media

"Inevitably, the Church's evangelizing mission too is deeply affected by the impact of the mass media. Since the mass media have an ever increasing influence even in remote areas of Asia, they can assist greatly in the proclamation of the Gospel to every corner of the continent." *(Ecclesia in Asia, n. 48)*

5.8 Church in India already has a good communication establishment and network

In spite of many odds and difficulties, the Church owns many well established communication centres, excellent training institutes, well accepted publications and above all scores of trained and committed media persons and professionals both in the church sector and secular media. Besides there are good Catholic press and Catholic publishing houses, radio and television production centres, institutes for performing arts, offices for public information and media relations, institutes and programs for training in and about media, media research, and Church-related organizations of communication professionals viz. Signis India and the Catholic Press Association of India.

6. Inspiration

6.1 The Triune God is a God of communication

"The Triune God is a God of communication. Our faith teaches us that God is not a solitary individual in lonely isolation. Rather, He is a trinity of persons in deep inter-personal communion. Creation is one form of his communication outside of Himself. Further, He communicates Himself to humanity to build a community of love amongst all peoples. He spoke through the prophets and others in preparation for the full communication in His Son, Jesus Christ. "In ancient times God spoke to our ancestors in many and various ways through the prophets, but in these last days he has spoken to us through his Son. (Heb. 1:1-2a)." *(CBCI GBM '04, n. 5)*

6.2 Jesus communicated the fullness of life

"Jesus Christ came to communicate the fullness of life so that all could have "life, and have it in abundance" (Jn. 10:10). He was in constant communication with people. His success in communication depended on his personal witness. While proclaiming his message of love he, the ever compassionate Saviour, adapted it to suit the people, particularly the poor and the marginalized." *(CBCI GBM '04, n. 6)*

6.3 Disciples are commissioned to witness and proclaim

"The disciples of Jesus are commissioned to 'go and proclaim the good news to all nations' (Mt 28:19). This commission implies communicating the whole person of Jesus, His word, His life, His message of Redemption. The most important and most effective means of communication is the WITNESS of personal holiness and an authentic life of discipleship. Taking into account our socio-political-economic-religious context, it also implies proclaiming Kingdom values in an inculturated manner for the transformation of the world." *(CBCI GBM '04, n. 7)*

7. Aims of Social Communication

7.1 Unity and advancement of all peoples

"Media, we recognize, are 'gifts of God' to humanity. They are in 'accordance with his design to unite people in fellowship' and help them 'to cooperate with his plan for their salvation' and work for the 'unity and advancement of all peoples. (*Communio et Progressio*, n. 2)" *(CBCI GBM '04, n. 4)*

7.2 Advancement of the plan of salvation

"The Church sees these media as 'gifts of God', which in accordance with his providential design, unite them in brotherhood and so help them to cooperate with his plan for their salvation." (*Communio et Progressio*, n. 2)

7.3 Fostering well-being of society

"The Church stresses the responsibility of media to contribute to the authentic, integral development of persons and to foster the well being of society. 'The information provided by the media is at the service of the common good. Society has a right to information based on truth, freedom, justice and solidarity." *(Ethics in Advertising, n.1)*

7.4 Respect for the right to information and duty to seek information, which should lead to better relationship, openness and sharing, culminating in communion.

"Modern man cannot do without information that is full, consistent, accurate and true... With the right to be informed goes the duty to seek information. Information does not simply occur; it has to be sought. On the other hand, in order to get it, the man who wants information must have access to the varied means of social communication. In this way, he can freely choose whatever means best suit his needs both personal and social. It is futile to talk about the right to information if a variety of the sources for it are not made available." (*Communio et Progressio*, n. 34)

7.5 Formation of Christians

"It is the Church's birthright to use and own any of these media which are necessary or useful for the formation of Christians and for pastoral activity. Pastors of soul have the task of instructing and directing the faithful how to use these media in a way that will ensure their own salvation and perfection and that of all mankind." (*Inter Mirifica*, n. 3)

7.6 To accomplish the evangelizing mission

"In more recent times the Church has considered even the instruments of social communication as providential means for the accomplishment of its mission to 'preach from the housetops' (*Lk* 12, 3), 'to all nations' (*Mk* 16, 15), 'to the end of the earth' (*Acts* 1, 8), the word of salvation." *(To the Training of Future Priests Concerning the Instruments of Social Communication, n. 3)*

8. Identity of Christian communicators

8.1 Inspired by Christ

"Inspired by the life and teachings of Jesus Christ, Christian communicators build a new society based on love and service." *(FABC BM 2000)*

8.2 Faithful to the Gospel

"The Christian communicator should move freely in different ways of communicating and be able to balance the use of the media of communications according to the call of the Gospel." *(FABC BM, 2000)*

8.3 Credible and relevant

"The Christian communicator must become a credible and relevant messenger of the Good News." *(FABC BM, '01)*

8.4 Constantly dialoguing with peoples and cultures

"Christian communicators by their witness and actions, enter into dialogue with peoples and cultures through social communications." *(FABC BM '97)*

8.5 Promoter of human dignity

"Convinced that all human beings are created in the image and likeness of the divine and have equal dignity, Christian communicators engage themselves promoting human dignity and human rights, more especially of the marginalized and neglected sections of the society." *(FABC BM '99)*

9. Guiding principles for the pastoral plan

9.1 God-centred and Asian in values

"Christian communication must help to keep God and bring Him back into the centre of human life, which corresponds very much with Asian values." (*Ecclesia in Asia*, 29)

9.2 Promoting common good

"The total output of the media in any given area should be judged by the contribution it makes to the common good. Its news, culture and entertainment should meet the growing needs of society." (*Communio et Progressio*, n. 16)

9.3 Fostering a people-oriented communication

"To be aware of the fact that secular media in our countries are not always people-oriented, liberating and contributing to a healthy development, this calls on the Church to make a serious move towards an *alternative*, culture-based, indigenous and people-oriented communication." *(FABC BM, '97)*

9.4 Promoting a communication that empowers people

"Empowering people with knowledge and skills in all forms of communications and making communications play an active role in all aspects of the Church's work."

9.5 Integrating the Good News into the new media culture

"It is not enough to use the media simply to spread the Christian message and the Church's authentic teaching. It is necessary to integrate that message into the 'new culture' created by modern communications." *(Redemptoris Missio, n. 37, Ecclesia in Asia, n. 48)*

9.6 Fostering an alternative culture

"Against the dominance of a 'consumer culture,' Christian communicators should help to build alternate cultures based on a deep and communicating spirituality." *(FABC BM, '99)*

10. Structure

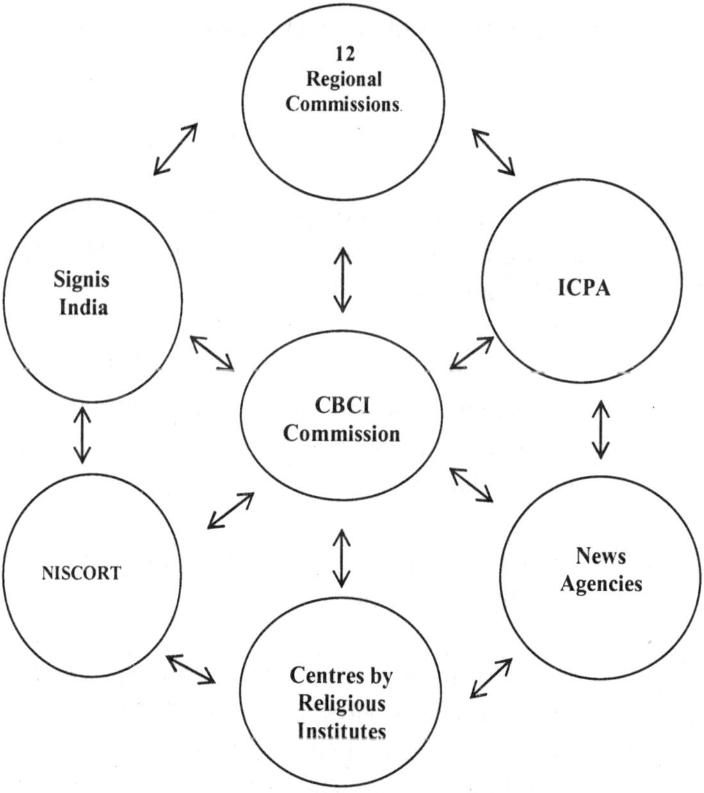

11. National Commission for Social Communications

11.1 National (CBCI) Commission shall consist of the following:

11.1.1 Bishop Chairman and Bishop Members elected by the CBCI General Body Meeting.

11.1.2 Executive Secretary

11.1.3 Co-opted Consulters

11.2 Job description of the Executive Secretary

11.2.1 Maintaining regular contact with the Commission chairman and members.

11.2.2 Coordinating the work of the Regional Commissions.

11.2.3 To share within India the directives and guidelines regarding social communication by the Holy See, the FABC and the CBCI.

11.2.4 To keep the Bishops of India and the Catholics informed regarding all developments in the field of social communication, particularly those affecting the Indian Church.

11.2.5 To help and support national and regional councils in the establishment of media offices.

11.2.6 In coordination with national and regional media offices, to devise ways and means of adapting the means of social communication to support evangelization and the ministries of the Church.

11.2.7 Preparing annual report and annual budget in consultation with the Chairman, responsible for the implementation of the projects/ programmes of the Commission.

11.2.8 Networking and coordinating the activities of the Media Organizations.

11.2.9 Fostering international relations and cooperation with other international organizations even beyond the Church.

11.2.10 Maintaining contacts with secular professionals and training institutions which would help people to become trained beyond the Church environment.

11.2.11 Facilitating/ organizing the diverse activities of the Commission.

11.2.12 Running the CBCI Media Office, maintaining and updating the CBCI Website and taking care of the Media Documentation and Research Section.

11.2.12 Working in collaboration with other Commissions of the CBCI.

12. Catholic Media Organizations and Institutes

12.1 While maintaining their professional and operational autonomy, the Catholic Media Organizations, the National Institutes of Training and the Catholic News Agencies will work in tandem with the CBCI Commission for Social Communications as per the spirit of this Pastoral Plan.

12.2 In order to facilitate a better coordination among the different Catholic Media Organizations, the National Communications Institutes and the Catholic News Agencies, the main Office Bearers and the CBCI Commission for Social Communications would meet at least once a year.

12.3 Each of the above Organizations and institutes would kindly prepare an annual report of their activities and present the same to the Chairman of the Commission by the end of each calendar year. Using these reports, the Commission Office would prepare a Consolidated Annual Report of the Catholic Communications Apostolate in India.

13. The Regional Commissions for Communications

The regional commissions would be on the pattern of the CBCI Commission and adapted as per the regional situation.

13.1 The Regional Commissions shall consist of the following:

13.1.1 Bishop Chairman and
Bishop Members elected by the Regional Bishops' Council.

13.1.2 Executive Secretary

13.1.3 Co-opted Consulters

13.2 Job description of the Executive Secretary

13.2.1 Maintaining regular contact with the Commission chairman and Commission members.

13.2.2 Coordinating the work of the diocesan Commissions in the region.

13.2.3 Preparing annual report and annual budget in consultation with the Chairman, responsible for the implementation of the projects/ programmes of the Commission.

13.2.4 Networking and coordinating the activities of the Media Organizations in the region.

13.2.5 Working in collaboration with the CBCI Commission.

14. Diocesan Commissions for Communications

14.1 Diocesan Commissions for Communications:

"The diocesan Bishop would constitute the diocesan Commission with a 'team of capable and qualified persons. With this in view, appropriate personnel – priests, religious and laypeople - should be identified and appointed. The team would do well to enlist the services of experts in the field of communications and other relevant areas. This will help to reach a wider public beyond ecclesiastical circles.'" *(CBCI GBM '04, n. 10)*

14.2 Job description for the diocesan director for communication

14.2.1 Provide media support to every ministry of the diocese. See that media support is planned into the various apostolates.

14.2.2 With this view, will organize a pastoral communication course for the various ministries with the help of the regional secretary for communications.

14.2.3 Will set up a media resource unit (MRU) at the diocesan headquarters to make available audiovisual materials useful to the diocese.

14.2.4 Will provide training in media education, communication skills and pastoral communication to various groups in the diocese.

14.2.5 When necessary, will produce/make available audio-visuals aids for the local use.

14.2.6 In collaboration with others concerned, will organize periodically a cultural media festival to enable Catholics to learn Scriptures, catechism etc., in the local cultural forms. This could also be in the form of competitions.

14.2.7 Will help to publish the diocesan magazine, supplying news from every ministry in the diocese that the people know of what is happening in the diocese.

14.2.8 Will periodically visit the Mission Stations to
a) see the effectiveness of devotional music broadcasted.
b) find out other media needs.

14.2.9 Will establish relations with the local media bodies, so that the Church's position on various issues is clearly articulated to them. Knowledge of how to prepare a proper press release is important. Periodically will present programme on local television and radio on issues important to the Church. Especially at Christmas and Easter, this can be done more easily.

14.2.10 Will work with local media bodies, especially NGOs.

14.2.11 Will, periodically give a written report to the bishop about ones activities. *(CBCI SCM, Bangalore, 1996)*

15. Conclusion

"We are grateful to God the 'giver of all good gifts' for the wonderful gifts of communications and for the creativity to use them imaginatively in His service and in the service of our country. We pray for his continued guidance to all media persons and communicators so that they are able to foster a new culture of communications, leading to a human family of peace and harmony." *(CBCI GBM '04, n. 20)*

The draft of the National Pastoral Plan for Communications was prepared by the CBCI Commission for Social Communications in consultation with many communicators from different parts of India. Then, it was revised at the National Conference on Communications participated by the members of the CBCI Commission, Chairmen Bishops of the Regional Commissions, Regional Secretaries, and office bearers of the Catholic Media Organizations. Later it was approved by the CBCI Standing Committee, during it's meeting, September 15 – 17, 2004, Bangalore.

Fr Henry D'Souza
Executive Secretary

Mission of the Communication Offices

"It is the mission of the national and diocesan offices to stimulate, promote and harmonize Catholic activities in the field of social communications. They will take particular pains about the training of the faithful, clerical and lay, by means of organized courses, conferences, study sessions and critical assessments prepared by their experts, so that the faithful, can use their own informed judgment. The offices will also be ready to give advice to producers engaged in the films, performances or broadcasts that concern religious subjects."

(Communio et Progressio, n. 170)

2

CALLED TO BE A COMMUNICATING CHURCH

Final Statement of the 26th CBCI General Body Meeting, Trichur 2004

Urgency of the Communications Apostolate

"All the members of the Church should make a concerted effort to ensure that the means of communication are put at the service of the multiple forms of the apostolate without delay and as energetically as possible, where and when they are needed. They should forestall projects likely to prove harmful, especially in those regions where moral and religious progress would require their intervention more urgently".

(Inter Mirifica, n. 13)

CALLED TO BE A COMMUNICATING CHURCH

We 156 members of the Catholic Bishops' Conference of India met at Marymatha Major Seminary, Trichur, Kerala, from Jan 07 -14, 2004 to reflect on the topic: The Church and Social Communications.

1. India we realize is making great strides in the field of Information Technology. The press, radio, cinema, television and other Information Technologies have expanded tremendously in the last few years. These have enabled people to relate and communicate to each other even when separated by long distances, thus building a world-wide web. The media are exercising a great influence on the minds of the people and creating public opinion.

2. We are happy to note that the mainstream mass media in India, by and large, have contributed greatly to uphold democratic and secular values. In the face, at times, of intense pressure from opposing forces, they have striven to safeguard the rights of citizens, particularly of the weaker sections and the minorities. We express our gratitude to the media

for contributing substantially to liberate our society from the dark forces of caste & communal hatred, corruption and crime. We salute those who have stood firm in a world of market forces, refusing to surrender to sensationalism, trivialization or to the fanning of social hatred. They have demonstrated that media have a prophetic role, indeed a vocation: to "speak out against the false gods and ideals of the day–materialism, hedonism, consumerism and narrow nationalism." *(Ethics in Communications, n.31)*

3. While the media bring information, education, and entertainment and create public opinion, they also have some negative influences. Some of the values propagated by the media are contrary to the Gospel and to our culture. An increase in violence can sometimes be traced to the influence of media. Family life, in particular, has been profoundly affected with the promotion of consumerism and values opposed to the sacredness of marriage being beamed into the home.

4. Media, we recognize, are 'gifts of God' to humanity. They are in "accordance with his design to unite people in fellowship" and help them "to cooperate with his plan for their salvation" and work for the "unity and advancement of all peoples" *(Communio et Progressio, n. 2)*. The signs of the times would demand that we all be media conscious. While encouraging people to be media users, the Church must dutifully alert our people to the threats being posed by the present mass-media and educate them, particularly children and youth, to use the media for authentic and wholesome lives in accordance with the plan of God. We need to motivate all our Church personnel to actively participate in the new opportunities created by media and the information technology to share the Good News and spread the Kingdom of God by fighting the menace of crime, corruption and communalism.

I. Called to Communicate

5. The Triune God is a God of communication. Our faith teaches us that God is not a solitary individual in lonely isolation. Rather, He is a trinity of persons in deep inter-personal communion. Creation is one form of his communication outside of Himself. Further, He communicates Himself to humanity to build a community of love amongst all peoples. He spoke through the prophets and others in preparation for the full communication in His Son, Jesus Christ. "In ancient times God spoke to our ancestors in many and various ways through the prophets, but in these last days he has spoken to us through his Son." (Heb. 1:1-2a).

6. Jesus Christ came to communicate the fullness of life so that all could have "life, and have it in abundance" (Jn. 10:10). He was in constant communication with people. His success in communication depended on his personal witness. While proclaiming his message of love he, the ever compassionate Saviour, adapted it to suit the people, particularly the poor and the marginalized.

7. The disciples of Jesus are commissioned to 'go and proclaim the good news to all nations' (Mt 28:19). This commission implies communicating the whole person of Jesus, His word, His life, His message of Redemption. The most important and most effective means of communication is the WITNESS of personal holiness and an authentic life of discipleship. Taking into account our socio-political-economic-religious context, it also implies proclaiming Kingdom values in an inculturated manner for the transformation of the world.

II. A Pastoral Plan for Communications

8. Social Communications have a significant role to play in every aspect of the Church's mission, and hence they must be

integrated into every Church ministry. A Pastoral Plan for Social Communications should become an integral part of the mission of the Church. We request that the CBCI Commission for Social Communications to draw up a Pastoral Plan, which would include a vision and strategies to stimulate, inspire and promote Catholic activities in this field. Thereby, the whole apostolate of the media will be 'placed under a single, overall direction' *(Communio et Progressio, n. 169)*.

9. It is recommended that as a first step an evaluation be made of existing Communication Centres and their activities. We need to rejuvenate our diocesan Commissions and Communications Centres so that they become truly institutions which communicate and network with local Christian media professionals and other like-minded persons, providing them with pastoral assistance.

10. As soon as possible every region/diocese should setup an Office for Social Communications, and prepare a Pastoral Plan for Communications. Every region/diocese in the country should appoint a director for Communications and a team of capable and qualified persons. With this in view, appropriate personnel – priests, religious and laypeople - should be identified and appointed. The team would do well to enlist the services of experts in the field of communications and other relevant areas. This will help to reach a wider public beyond ecclesiastical circles.

11. The mainstream media, both national and regional, play a vital role in informing the public and creating a public opinion. While upholding the legitimate rights of the media, the Church needs to network with the mainstream media to highlight people's concerns and the Church's point of view. It is necessary to cultivate good relations with media personal. From time to time they can be invited for a friendly dialogue and fellowship. Realising that the regional media

in particular have at times not been too favourable to the Church, we must give greater attention to the regional media, both print and electronic. We need to identify and train people for this work.

12. Every diocese should have a talented and trained spokesperson who can establish links at different levels – deanery/ diocesan/ regional/ national.

13. A special area of concern for us is the influence of media on the family. Relevant programmes should be evolved to make the children, youth and parents appreciative, critical and discerning consumers of media.

14. While we deeply appreciate the work done by the Catholic media in spite of scant resources and many odds, we realize the need of improving our periodicals, publications and media productions by bringing in more professionalism in order to make them truly communicative.

15. A large section of the society is illiterate and is not reached by modern media. Care is to taken not to neglect these sections, the least and the last, of society. Hence, the importance of developing systematically, seriously and purposefully alternate media such as folk arts, dance, drama, music, *keertan*, *katha*, street-plays, Christmas cribs, Passion scenes etc.

16. Recognizing that 'Communications Day' is a valuable opportunity to sensitize the community, the Sunday before the feast of Christ the King should be celebrated as 'India Communications Day' with a meaningful liturgy and relevant programmes. The Holy Father's message for the day could be disseminated to the grassroots even beyond the Church through the secular media.

III. Communications Training

17. If a pastoral plan is to be successfully implemented, a proper formation programme should be arranged for all in the Church. All leaders of the community - bishops, priests, religious and lay leaders - should get adequate training in communications so that they can effectively discharge their duties for evangelization and defense of the genuine interests of the Church and society.

18. Seminary formators, future diocesan and religious priests should be adequately formed to proclaim the Word effectively and celebrate the Sacred Mysteries meaningfully. Efforts must be made to improve their communication skills. A proper media course should be part of the seminary curriculum. We urge that communications be integrated into all formation – biblical, catechetical and other.

19. Our dedicated catechists, teachers, leaders in our parishes and religious institutions, social workers, and health personnel are living agents of communication to the public. So also, we are aware how important is the role of those in offices and government duties, especially those in politics - the Lord has placed on them a great responsibility, indeed! We encourage all these to get adequate training to communicate the Gospel more effectively. With a view to the future, we must identify and encourage creative young talented persons to pursue a profession in the media.

IV. Conclusion

20. We are grateful to God the "giver of all good gifts" for the wonderful gifts of communications and for the creativity to use them imaginatively in His service and in the service of our country. We pray for his continued guidance to all media persons and communicators so that they are able to foster a new culture of communications, leading to a human family of peace and harmony.

Jan. 14, 2004, Marymatha Major Seminary, Trichur.

PART II

3

CALLED TO BE A *COMMUNICATING* CHURCH
Some Reflections for Planning

***Fr Franz-Josef Eilers**, svd*
Executive Secretary, FABC-OSC

Need to Integrate that Message into the New Culture

"However, 'it is not enough to use the media simply to spread the Christian message and the Church's authentic teaching. It is necessary to integrate that message into the 'new culture' created by modern communications.'"

(Ecclesia in Asia n. 48)

CALLED TO BE
A *COMMUNICATING* CHURCH
Some Reflections For Planning

Fr Franz-Josef Eilers, svd

Instead of commenting on single parts of the final document of the CBCI meeting on communication in January 2004 let me make some basic remarks which should help to have a sufficient grounding and perspective for different activities and concerns.

1. When the Vatican II document "*Inter Mirifica*" was presented to the Council fathers 1962 it had right in the beginning a footnote which proposed to use the expression "*Social Communication*". Following a suggestion of the late Fr. Enrico Baragli, sj the preparatory commission for the document proposed this new expression because they felt that names like mass media, media of diffusion, audio-visual media would not be sufficient to express fully the concern of the Church in the field of communication. This was unanimously accepted without further detailed discussion and the expression became the official 'label' for the Church's communication activities.

Later Italian scholar Giorgio Braga described *social* communication as the "study of communicative processes within society" which according to him is based on a sociology which puts communication at the centre of the life of a society (1). Simply *social* communication can be defined as the communication *of* and *in* human society. Media and mass media are in this consideration only *one* part, though an important one of the total of communicative expressions. *Social Communication* includes *all* ways and means of human communication in society from interpersonal to group, media and cyberspace communication.

Unfortunately this broader perspective of communication seems not to be reflected that much in the mind of people and even not in relevant Church documents though it has important consequences for any communications apostolate of the Church: It starts with the inter-personal communication of Church members and is in the first instance not a question of technical means. The communication of the early Church as reflected in the *Acts of the Apostles* covered in a relatively short time the whole of the Mediterranean world without any special technical means. The people themselves were the ones who through their life, their testimony and their behaviour convinced others to join the community of believers. *Social* Communication starts and includes all of this which reflects also the personal faith, conviction, spirituality of individuals and community experience. It also includes the culture- specific ways and means of communicating like storytelling, drama, dance, music and other ways of communication to nourish community and relationships.

2. There is an additional consideration pointing in the same direction from the emerging field of *Communication Theology*. In the past we very often tried to develop a "Theology of Communication" which somehow wanted to "baptize" communication, especially mass media communication and bring it into the Church's fold.

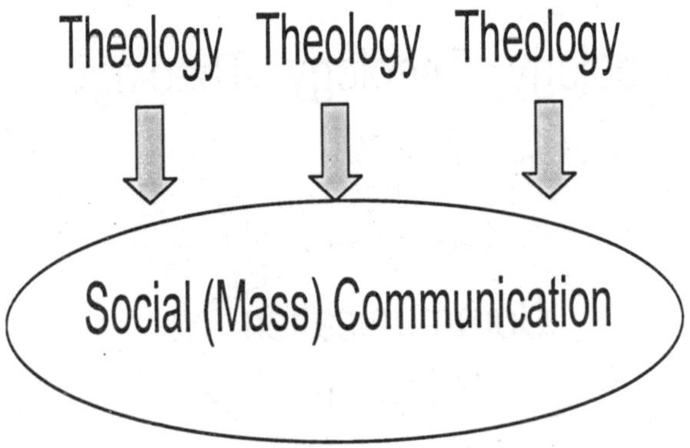

There is also the consideration for a "Communicative Theology" which is concerned about the 'communicative expressions' of Theology, where Theology expresses itself in such a way that it can be more easily understood.

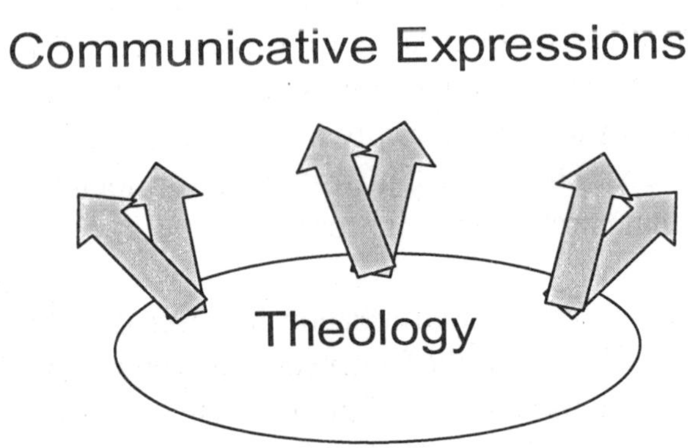

"Communication Theology", however, takes Communication as a theological principle. The whole of Theology is considered and studied under the perspective of communication (2):

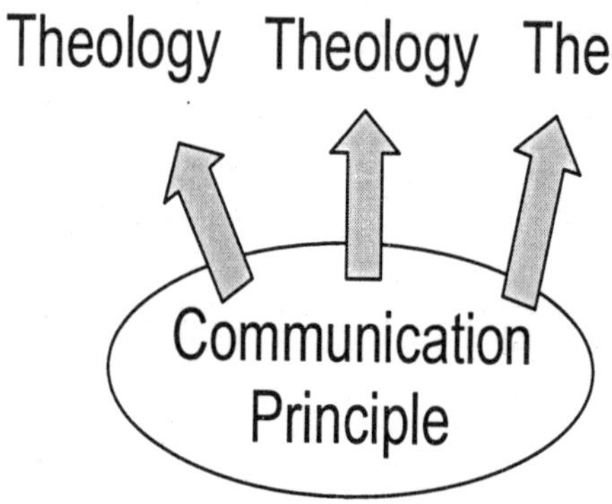

a. The Trinitarian God communicates in Himself i.e. there is an ongoing communication at the Centre of the Holy Trinity, Father, Son and Holy Spirit communicating with each other and we as human beings are able to communicate because we are created in "His image and likeness". Here is the theological reason for our own communication ability.

b. This Trinitarian communicating God, however, also reveals himself in communicating with his creatures. He uses all ways and means of human communication; he communicates verbally and non-verbally, he communicates with signs and actions. The whole Old Testament is a document of God's communication with his people.

c. The high point of this revelation, however, is the Incarnation of Jesus Christ. God the Father communicates with his creatures through his son, Jesus Christ. As the letter to the Hebrews affirms: "In the past God spoke to our forefathers through the prophets at many times and in various ways. But in these last days he has spoken to us by his son, whom he appointed heir of all things, and through whom he made the universe. The son is the radiance of God's glory and the exact representation of his being..." (Heb.1, 1-3). Jesus Christ again communicates in words and deeds, he uses signs and symbols which go beyond or support his words. He communicates through the whole way of his life. (cf. *Communio et Progressio,* n. 11).

d. From all this the Church receives her sending to communicate. She is to continue God's communication in Revelation and Incarnation into the here and now of every time. Thus the Church is the presence of the communicating God between people; she is – as Avery Dulles titled a famous paper for the American Bishops already in 1971 – Communication. Thus social communication is not just a job for specialists, even Church-specialists, but a dimension for every Christian as member of the Church and to be reflected in daily life. In the same way like in the *Acts of the Apostles* also today every Christian is and must be a communicator in the full sense thus reflecting the Church.

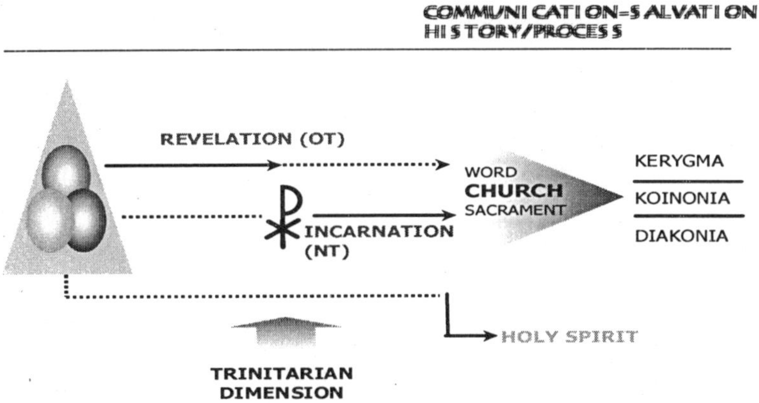

If Jesus is the example and the content of the Trinitarian God's communication with his people he should also be the central example for any Christian. And how did Jesus communicate? He did it through his way of life, but in a special way through his invitation for the Kingdom of God. There are three basic steps in his communication which are also the basic steps for any human communication. It can be exemplified in the story of the healing of the mother-in-law of Peter as reported in Mark 1, 31: Jesus "went to hear, took her hand and helped her up". This means in our communication we go to the person concerned, put ourselves into her/his situation and lift him/her up. These steps can be found in many of Jesus' healing activities like e.g. also in the healing of the leper in Mt. 8, 1-4: "Jesus stretched out his hand, touched him and healed him: I do choose, be made clean!"

Any Christian communication needs these same three steps, which then can further be applied to the Church as an institution. (3)

3. All Christian Communication has two dimensions: *ad intra* and *ad extra* and every planning has right from the outset be clear which kind of communication or audience is wanted. Do we want to communicate inside the Christian community to our members or to people outside? In communicating to the outside the first question, however, is not about ways and means or methodologies and 'tricks' to be used to 'catch' so to say the interest and eye of people. All communication to the outside must be based on and reflect proper communication inside the community. If the Christian community lives and practices the basic steps of Christian communication as Jesus lived them then they will be a 'fire' which shines from within which is reflected indirectly or directly in any communication to the outside. In the early Church it was the statement: "See, how the love each other" which attracted people. The same holds good for today. This is, however, a question of spirituality and a convincing witness of life of the members of the Church.

Last year the Indian communication scholar Dharm P.S. Bhawuk published an article in the "International Journal of Intercultural Relations" (4) with the title: "Culture's influence on creativity: the case of Indian spirituality. In this presentation he shows in a convincing way how spirituality is at the basis of Indian culture. He even gives under the historic perspectives a "list of Indian saints and gurus" from 600 BC till 1990 (5) and continues to write about "modern innovations in Spirituality". Should this emphasis on spirituality not also be an essential part of our approach in Christian communication? At the University of Santo Tomas in Manila we developed a few years ago a "Christian Communication model" which is not patterned after the usual Sender-Message-Receiver approach where the message, the word of God, stays central. The messenger is just an instrument in the hands of the Lord and is only as good as s/he reflects and lives the message. The messenger is nothing and the word of God, the message is everything (6).

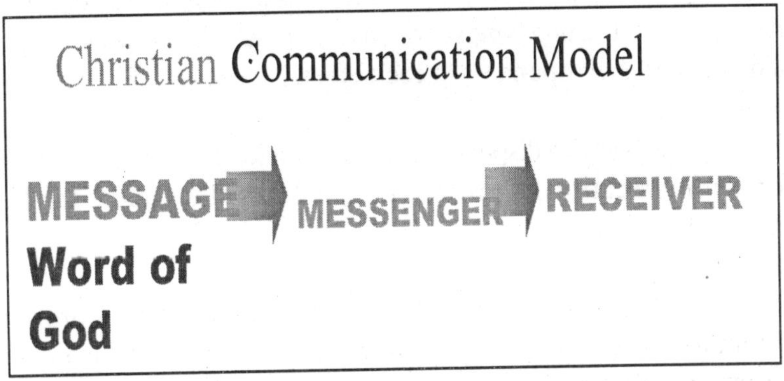

Such a disposition is essential also for all Church attempts in Public Communication/ Relations. Especially in a country like India where Christians are a very small minority it is important to be aware of the need for a public image of the Church as a loving and committed community. Law suites between Christians submitted to secular courts are definitely counter productive in this perspective. Also the sometimes tense relations between different groups of Christians, but also between bishops and clergy, clergy and laity, between different rites or other faith communities are a counter testimony to real Christian communication which leads to love and understanding and healing like the communication of Jesus.

We just finished on July 9, 2004 in Manila a four day congress and retreat fore some 4000 priests of the Philippines. They all were housed in individual families who volunteered to give them board, breakfast and dinner every day. All went home strengthened in the experience of community and challenge, but also in a testimony for the bond between laity and priests.

Communication ad *intra* starts with the interpersonal communication but then goes through the experience of community like e.g. in parishes, but also basic Christian communities and other smaller groupings to the bigger presentations of Church. It is reflected in the personal trusting bond between bishops and their priests, clergy and laity and their openness to each other.

Out of such a disposition also the challenges and possibilities for communication *ad extra* to people from other faiths can be managed.

4. From all this arises the essential need for a proper communication ability of Church leaders and those who aspire to become one of them like our seminarians. It is not so much what we *do* but rather what we *are*! This again is a question of deep personal and communal spirituality. Communication formation has to start with the essentials of human / Christian communication e.g. in the seminary and church organizations. It is the need for a total openness to God, to self and to others, which must be developed.(7) For the seminary the role of the Spiritual Director in such a process is of special importance if the relationship with the directee is really based on total openness with each other. If a seminarian or religious has learned to face his/her issues, reflect and address them, s/he will become free and is open and available to others. This is a formation which everybody needs who wants to become a good communicator. This will determine the way we talk and deal with each other. If I am settled with myself I will be open to others and willing to listen with all my capabilities because I do not need this 'energy' any more for myself.

Such a disposition creates also within a community the spirit of mutual support and understanding. Recently Tony Fernandez, the founder of the successful first Asian low cost airline *Air Asia* was asked in an interview: "What is most central to your success?" and he answered: "My staff are my greatest asset. I know every one of them by name and we all share the same passion. I pay them well and we're transparent. We close our booth at midnight and have meetings after that. We discuss everything – our low and high points. There have been few low points till now" (8). Can we as Church honestly make similar statements e. g. for our dioceses, parishes or other Church institutions?

If after acquiring this basic communication disposition which everybody needs someone has special interests and talents in communication s/he should be promoted for further and more specialized training as is proposed by the Church documents (9).

5.

a. The basics for a *specialized training* in communication can be given in some Church institutions with training courses different parts of the country and with different kinds of specialization. For a deeper and more professional training, however, the many existing academic institutions in the country should be tapped and used. I did my own communication studies and doctorate in a State

University which not only brought me quality but also the friendship with some companions who later became famous academicians or public figures in the field. Such an academic training would also give the Church a certain professional standing in countries where she is a small minority.

b. There is also a need for training in a more general way through *Media/Communication Education*. Especially our young people growing up in a changing and globalized world with tremendous technical developments in communications need a proper and thorough guidance and education in and for communication. How can we help and prepare young people to meet the challenges of modern technologies, to handle the impact of the media and globalized communication? Do we offer such opportunities in our many catholic schools and other institutions of learning? Do we have enough properly trained staff to secure such training?

c. Very often social communication is seen as a field for specialized people and the attitude of many is: let the specialists do! In reality, however, everybody is a communicator and exposed to a communications world which is by now part of our daily lives. How do we act and re-act here? Yes we need Church structures and means for communication but probably more needed is a change of mindset in our people and especially in those responsible. This again is not only a question of training alone but also of the basic communication formation we spoke about above. Formation addresses the total person and goes deeper than training and skills. It refers to an inner disposition and ability which goes beyond skills.

Yes we need an evaluation of the status quo of our communication initiatives and institutions. But even before we properly plan more technical details we must be aware of the mindset of people and look for ways and means to change or adjust them.

6. Considering the many individual communication initiatives in the country it might be also good to be aware of the communication structures of the Church as reflected in the respective documents to set the right priorities and responsibilities. There is clearly a hierarchical structure which is to be supported by a – what I call – professional structure (10). Vatican II in *Inter Mirifica* does not leave any doubt about the final responsibility of the bishop for all communication activities in his diocese: "It is for bishops to oversee activities and projects of this sort in their own dioceses, to promote and, where they touch the public apostolate, to regulate them, including those under the control of exempt religious" (n. 20) This responsibility is further extended in the following text to the creation of national offices to be entrusted to "Episcopal Commissions or bishops appointed to do that task" (n. 21). *Communio et Progressio*, the pastoral instruction demanded by the council fathers later explained the obligations of the bishops further especially in their responsibility for pastoral planning (11).

The professional organizations like UCIP which in India would be the Indian Catholic Press Association and Signis are to complement and support the national office especially in their own field of specialization like Press or the electronic media. But we should be aware that there are also quite some concerns in the overall field of social communication which are not fully covered by these professional organizations.

It is along these lines that also the work of *Radio Veritas Asia* has to be mentioned. This only continental short wave radio station of the Church in the world was originally founded for broadcast into mainland China. Later other countries followed, especially those who did not have free access to radio in their own countries. Right from its beginning the bishops of the "Federation of Asian Bishops' Conferences" (FABC) took up the responsibility for·the operations and financing of the station whereas the legal responsibility is with the archbishop of Manila and a group of Filipino bishops as demanded by the laws of the country where foreigners can not be owners of such undertakings. There are programs in five Indian languages (Hindi, Tamil, Bengali, Telugu, and Urdu) which are daily broadcast from the Philippines. The major part of these programs is produced by production studios in the language areas which should be fully financed locally. These activities of RVA are a responsibility of the respective local bishops in cooperation with the FABC (12). It should be integral part of their planning including the training of qualified persons to also man the respective language studio in the headquarters in Manila. If because of new possibilities in India itself such language programs are not needed any more respective decisions should be made to save money and give the slots to other countries where there might be a greater need. We should remind ourselves also here on the words of Pope John Paul II in the section on Social Communication of *Ecclesia in Asia* (n. 48) where he says: "I echo the Synod Fathers' commendation of *Radio Veritas Asia*, to only continent-wide radio station for the Church in Asia, for its almost thirty years of evangelization through broadcasting. Efforts must be made to strengthen this excellent instrument of mission, through appropriate language programming, personnel and financial help from Episcopal Conferences, and dioceses in Asia."

7. Since India is one of the fastest growing countries in Internet technology we probably should also more carefully look into the new possibilities given trough these new technologies. We are still in the stage of tests and searching for the different possibilities the new medium gives. It can be used as documentation where the Church presents what she is and does to an interested public. The Internet, however, can not fully answer personal questions and needs but it

can lead to a deeper understanding or show ways how and through whom to reach it. The Net gives through E-Mail and similar means new and quick ways to contact and inform each other. Even meetings can be opened to a greater interested public through posting their presentations or even streaming their procedures. The prayers of the Church can be opened for those interested to join; meditative and liturgical reflections and proposals can be made available up to virtual classrooms for catechetical instruction and other courses with a tutor and participants from the whole country and beyond. The Internet further can animate to visit Churches and shrines, and can invite people to participate in services like in the old times the bells from the Church tower invited the faithful (13).

The Net is in a growing way used by Protestant and especially fundamentalist groups for 'E-vangelism" with "Cyber-missionaries". Maybe we could set up together with the mainstream Protestants a special study centre to collect and process information and experiences. Bangalore is considered the cyber-city of India. Not only is there the St. Peter's Pontifical Institute with a communications department but also the Protestant United Theological College with recognized MA and PhD programs. This could be developing into a service beyond India for the Church at large especially in Asia. We are aware, of course, that up till now not all but only certain groups especially in urban areas have access to the Net. But this will change rapidly e.g. with new devices not dependent on phone lines and wires anymore. We should not loose track!

8. Since the final document of the CBCI meeting repeats the proposal of Church documents to integrate communication "into every Church ministry" let me finally present to you the four possible approaches which I developed in my classes (14). From this it might become more clear where we stand and where we want to go.

These approaches can be illustrated in the following way, which should be self-evident:

APPROACHES TO SOCIAL COMMUNICATION MINISTRY: PLANNING & ACTIVITIES

1. Isolation Approach

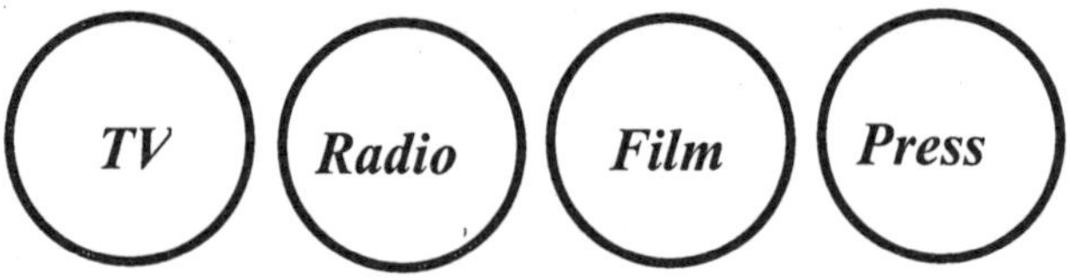

2. Unifying Approach

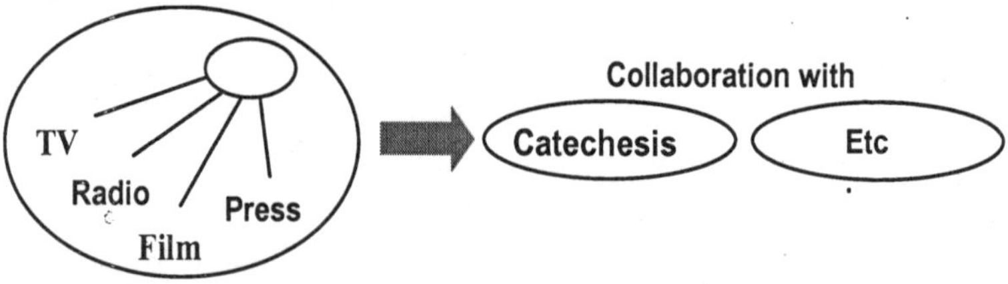

3. Basic Collaborative Approach

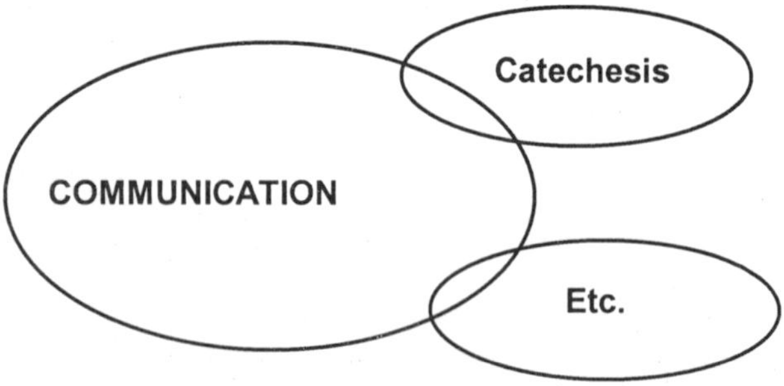

4. Integral Dimension Approach

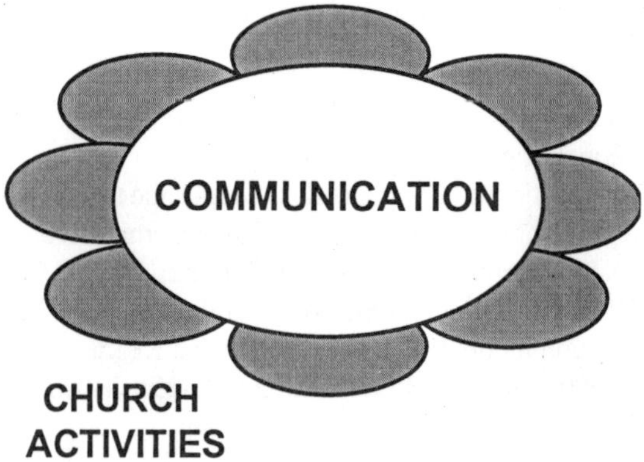

These approaches are indicating different steps in the relationship between communication and other Church ministries. They should help to analyze but also to consider, planning and executing the communication dimension in all ministries. It should help to see were we are now and where we want to go.

[Fr. Franz Josef Eilers, svd belongs to the Congregation of the Divine Word and presently is the Executive Secretary of the FABC OSC. He is professor for Social Communication and Missiology at the Divine Word School of Theology in Tagatay City (Philippines). He also teaches at the University of Sto. Tomas for an MA Theology Program in School / Pastoral Communication. He has been teaching at the Gregorian and Salesian Universities in Rome and in other places and Consultor of the Pontifical Council for Social Communications.]

Notes

(1) cf. Franz-Josef Eilers: Communicating in Community. Third revised and enlarged edition. Manila (Logos) 2002, p. 313 ff. Indian Edition Indore (Satprakashan Sanchar Kendra) 1996, p. 271 ff

(2) For further details cf. Franz-Josef Eilers: Communicating in Ministry and Mission. Second Edition, Manila (Logos) 2004; Indian Edition Bangalore

(Asian Trading) 2004, p. 17 - 29. cf also Eilers 2002, 41-60

(3) Ibid. 2004 p. 69 - 71

(4) Vol. 27: 2003, pp. 1-22

(5) Ibid. p.7

(6) Eilers 2004, p. 68; 150 f.

(7) Cf. Eilers 2004 p.31-36

(8) The Nation, Bangkok, May 10, 2044

(9) See: Congregation for Catholic Education: Guide to the Training of future Priests concerning the Instruments of Social Communication from March 19, 1986. In: Franz-Josef Eilers (ed.) Church and Social Communication. Basic Documents. Second Edition. Manila (Logos) 1997, pp. 177-198. Indian Edition Indore (Satprakashan Sanchar Kendra) 1996 pp. 163-184

(10) Cf. Eilers 2004, pp.79-84; Eilers 2003, pp. 245-251; Indian Ed. 1996 pp.219-226

(11) Eilers 2004, p. 123 ff.

(12) Cf. "Bandung Covenent" between RVA and the national Bishops' Conferences at the 5th FABC General Assembly, Bandung July 1990. In: RVA since 1969. Manila 1995 p. 43

(13) Cf. Ekkhart Bieger: Das Internet - Orakel oder Zeitung? Perspektiven fuer kirchliche Medienarbeit. In: Communicatio Socialis. Vol. 37, 2004 pp. 62-69

(14) Cf. Eilers 2004, pp. 129 ff.

•••

4

WAYS TO IMPROVE PROFESSIONALISM IN CATHOLIC PUBLICATIONS

4.1

HOW TO IMPROVE PROFESSIONALISM IN CATHOLIC PUBLICATIONS

Fr M.A. Joe Antony, sj

I do not think we need to answer the question why we need to be professional. We have crossed that stage long ago. I guess all of us are convinced about the need for professionalism. The recent Church documents have repeatedly talked of its necessity and value.

Before I make my suggestions on making our publications professional, we have to agree on what we understand by professionalism or a professional.

For our purpose, just one definition and one description may be enough.

First a definition taken from a Harvard University website:

"Professionalism is a set of characteristics or behaviours that are worthy of the high standards of an occupation that requires advanced training."

What may be more helpful is the description that comes from a keynote address at a Conference on Professionalism delivered by Tom De Marco, held in London, 1996.

He calls it a Four P-model because he says to deserve the epithet 'professional', one must have the following characteristics:

Professing: The individual must freely profess to choose and stay in the profession.

Permanent: The call of a professional is not momentary or temporary but permanent. He is permanently committed to this calling.

Proficient: A professional is proficient, does his job with an assured competence, with skill born of long practice.

Promise-keeping: Professionals make certain promises to themselves for the sake of their clients, who are, in our case, readers and keep these promises at all times. These are centred on the ethics related to the profession – the professional ethics. A professional will never stoop to do what is unethical, whatever may be the temptation or the provocation.

If we are committed to running our publications in a professional manner, what can we do concretely to achieve this aim?

I have grouped my suggestions according to the various 'actors' or 'players' involved. Some of these suggestions may be basic common sense, but I include them here simply because they are not followed.

1. The Editor

If you want professionalism, you need professionals. It is as simple as that. Therefore the editor of the Catholic periodical must be a professional. That means someone with at least P.G. Degree in Journalism from a good university and some basic experience.

As a professional, the editor should resolve that he will not yield to any demand or pressure from anyone to do something unprofessional. He must make sure that this is mentioned clearly in the contract he signs with the Proprietor. The periodical's professionalism may be judged by the fairness and impartiality with which the editor chooses and edits the material for publication.

As a professional committed to proficiency or excellence, he should constantly strive to update his knowledge and improve his skills.

Because permanence is a characteristic of professionalism, the editor should commit himself to stay in the job for a minimum of, say, 5-7 years. He should not abandon it the moment he finds greener pastures.

He constantly strives to serve the readers' interest by trying his best to offer them a periodical that they enjoy and benefit from and at the same time he fulfills the expectations of the proprietor by doing what he has committed himself to, in the contract. If he does it, one can reasonably hope that his magazine will soon be financially viable.

2. The Manager

A Catholic periodical requires professional management that includes budgeting, computerization of all data regarding subscriptions, advertisements, payments etc, strategies to attract new subscribers as well as to make the existing subscribers keep renewing their subscription.

In the case of most of our publications in India, the editor is also the manager. Whenever possible, it is good to keep these roles distinct, as the talents required for these two jobs are quite different. If the periodical cannot afford the salary for a professional manager, it must make sure the editor plays the role of a manager too effectively.

3. Proprietor

In the Indian scenario, to a large extent, the bishop of the place where the magazine is published happens to be the proprietor of the Catholic magazine; in some other cases it is the religious superior of a congregation. The proprietor should follow a professional approach in searching for and appointing and terminating the services of an editor.

a. The Search

Here we'll have to classify Catholic magazines according to their outlook and reach. A few magazines are national in their outlook and therefore their readers are scattered all over the country. Some are regional, and some are diocesan.

The professional way of looking for an editor for a national magazine is to initiate a nation-wide search for the best talent available in the country – similarly for a regional magazine the search should be extended to the entire state or region.

The proprietor will be acting in a totally unprofessional manner if he is going to limit his search just to his own diocese. One can't defend this by saying that the magazine belongs to the diocese.

If the diocese owns a paper that is national in its reach and outlook, the search too should be national. Obviously, if the best talent available in the country happens to be someone within his own diocese, his job obviously becomes easy.

Usually what prevents the bishop-proprietor from initiating a nation-wide search for the best talent available in the country?

Ironically, it may not even occur to him to do so. An unprofessional ostrich-like attitude does not let him look beyond his diocese. In some cases it could be one of the 'ism's that afflict most of us – regionalism or casteism or the new 'ism' which makes some diocesan bishops or clergy to be anti-religious or some religious to be anti-diocesan clergy. So the bishop looks for someone of his region or caste or diocese or a friend or a protege and completely ignores the good of the magazine and its readers. What he forgets is that he himself needs the best talent available to keep a national magazine fulfill its purpose, to satisfy the readers all over the country and to keep it financially viable. By not trying to find the best talent available, he is harming the long-term interests of the magazine he owns and betraying its readers all over the country and beyond.

Sometimes financial considerations make some bishop-proprietors limit their search to priests or sisters, and not to extend it to the laity. Because if you hire a lay person you'll have to give him a salary that is good enough to support him and his family, whereas if it is a priest or a religious, a modest remuneration will be enough.

b. The appointment

Since it is not easy for the proprietor to identify the best talent available in the country or region, the proprietor should leave it to a committee that has credibility and includes professionals.

Once someone is identified, the appointment should be made on the basis of a clearly-drafted contract. The contract may be initially for a probationary period of 1 or 2 years, when the editor and the proprietor see if they have what they were looking for.

In thc contract the proprietor of a Catholic magazine has a right to demand that the editor does not publish anything that goes against the Church dogma or moral teachings etc, but within those limits the editor has the right to demand complete editorial freedom. If both are satisfied during the probationary period, the editor should be appointed for a minimum period of 5 to 7 years.

There are several instances when editors have been forced to leave the magazine, with a lot of hurt and bitterness, because such guidelines were not followed.

c. Termination of services

At least one year before the term ends, both the editor and the proprietor should begin a dialogue about ending or renewing the contract. It is unfair and unprofessional to end the contract without giving enough time for the other. If the editor does it, the proprietor will not be in a position to initiate a new search all over again and find an appropriate person. If the proprietor does it, the editor will not have the time he needs to plan his future, explore and decide on other assignments.

3. The Regional Commission

If professionalism is recognized as a value which the Church needs to promote, what should naturally follow is the care and seriousness with which the bishops of the region choose the bishop to head the communication commission or council.

If possible, the first preference should obviously be someone who has been a full-time professional communicator. Obviously, this may not always be possible. Whenever it has been, it has yielded rich dividends. If there has been a lot of appreciation and welcome from communicators for the recent Vatican documents on communication, the primary reason is the person who heads the Pontifical Commission for Social Communication. Archbishop John Foley is a professional journalist. He was the editor of a Catholic periodical in the U.S. for a number of years.

But, as I said, this may not always be possible. Then the bishops should look for one who at least has had some experience and knowledge of this field. Once again whenever this is done, we have happy, commendable results. Tamil Nadu, whose situation I know well, can be a concrete example. Its present Regional Chairman for Communications is someone knowledgeable and experienced and therefore everyone can see the positive developments like a long term vision and detailed planning.

In order to make the diocesan publications that will come under it professional, the Regional Commission can play a role similar to what I suggest for the National Commission.

4. The National Commission

In order to safeguard and promote professionalism in our publications, I think that the National CBCI Commission for Social Communication should play a pro-active, supervisory role, at least for the major national and regional publications. I am not suggesting that the commission plays the role of a super-boss, sitting in Delhi and dictating terms. Rather, it should play the role of a respected guide, animator and co-ordinator. Sometimes it may be called to play the role of a mediator and on some rare occasions, even that of an arbitrator.

The Commission should speak up and mediate whenever an editor or a bishop-proprietor or a Regional Chairman is behaving in a blatantly unprofessional manner.

Conclusion

It is ironic and sad that most of those who are involved with Church media, in spite of living and working in the 21st century, still do not realize that it is the professional approach that serves everyone's interests. It is a professional approach that brings magazine subscribers, it is a professional approach that makes it financially viable, it is a professional approach that wins for the magazine a good name and reputation. It is a professional approach that earns for the editor and proprietor the readers' good will and gratitude. It is the professional approach that serves best the Church's mission.

An unprofessional approach is an insult and disservice to God whom we are trying to serve through the print media. If we run our periodicals in an unprofessional way, we are the modern counterparts of Cain, the brother of Abel, who offered to God things that were unworthy of Him.

[Fr. M.A Joe Antony, sj, is the Editor and Publisher of the New Leader, a leading national Catholic fortnightly published from Chennai. He is also the editor of Jivan, the magazine of South Asian Jesuits but read also by a lot of non-Jesuits including clergy, religious and laity in and outside South Asia.]

...

4.2

PROMOTING PROFESSIONALISM IN CATHOLIC PUBLICATIONS AND PRODUCTIONS

Fr Alphonse Elengikal, ssp

Introduction

As I was reflecting on the topic of our discussion, this morning, what came to my mind first was a chance meeting I had with a senior Editor in Goa, some time ago. I was introduced to him by one of his junior colleagues. As I found him quite relaxed and willing to talk, I took the chance to present him with a couple of copies of *The Teenager*, which I had with me. He really took a keen interest in the magazine and went through the copies. So, I ventured to ask him as to what he thought was the main reason for the poor circulation of Catholic periodicals including *The Teenager*.

The gentleman thought for a while, and then responded: "Your magazine and most of the so-called Catholic periodicals are far from being professional, inspite of possibly having a good content. He continued, "People rush to Catholic schools everywhere, inspite of knowing fully well that these are run by religious institutions and often headed by a priest or nun. The reason is this: most Catholic schools are professionally run, and efficient, too. But," he concluded, "Most Catholic periodicals, as far as I see, are simply not professional in most respects."

In as much as it was hard to take the message in, I know too well that what he said was true. Most secular publications are professionally run (we've for example, *Outlook, The Week, India Today*, etc) because they know otherwise they'll have to close down. On the other hand, most of the Catholic publications and products are not professional, and are not efficiently run because we don't have to struggle for survival, and we know we can go on, even incurring huge losses, every year! We don't allow ourselves to be challenged.

However, I would like to place before you a couple of copies of a periodical, which stands out as an exception to what is said above — *Famiglia Cristiana*, the Italian weekly founded by Blessed James Alberione almost 75 years ago. Fr Alberione saw the periodical reaching its zenith, as the largest circulated Catholic weekly in the world, and possibly as the largest-circulated periodical in the whole of Italy, a position it still maintains today with a circulation of over 1 million copies, every week. Fr Alberione insisted that the periodical maintain high professional standards all through. No wonder, while similar periodicals closed shop much earlier, *Famiglia Cristiana* goes on full swing!

Professionalism — what does it mean?

To induce professionalism in our publications and products,

we need to have a clear idea about the term itself. I see too many people confusing professionalism with commercialism. To my mind to be a professional means a lot more than being simply commercial which refers more to the motive of one's activity. While in commercialism monetary gains or profit-making becomes one's primary goal, professionalism goes far ahead; it calls for competence gained through training, knowledge and experience. Professionalism expects in a *professional* proper skills and efficiency, and in publications and products high standards and maximum appeal to the target group. It goes without saying that professionalism calls for a certain amount of good business sense and, more importantly, accountability. All this would mean having a business sense without being *highly* commercial, which makes one do things primarily for the sake of money or monetary gains. I would add to this a high degree of commitment to the cause of journalism and media ethics.

I would now like to vaguely classify most publications in India into 4 main categories:

1. Publications that are highly specialized and highly professional.
2. Publications that are highly commercial than professional.
3. Publications that combine professionalism with a good degree of commercialism.
4. Publications that do not fit into any of the above categories.

What is desirable in our case, at least according to me, is the *third* category. I believe the time has come for Catholic publications to be professional in every respect, even bringing in some amount of commercialism and financial viability.

1. This will mean that we should be able to target and reach a much broader section of the reading public with varying tastes

and interests, in our respective languages. I feel in today's context, we need to redefine the role of a Catholic periodical. It should be a healthy mix of "secular topics" and Church-related news and articles.

2. In the case of periodicals in particular, the above makes it mandatory that we have on our regular contributors list people who are competent and knowledgeable in different aspects of life. We need to bring in professional lay people into various sectors of the periodical.
3. Our products (particularly periodicals) should also maintain quality technically — this would mean an appealing cover, good paper, attractive layout, and when possible, multi-colour printing, and that we use professional methods in marketing our products.
4. Finally, I would like to say that our publications should never shy away from taking risks and demonstrating courage when required. Our readers expect this of us much more than we ordinarily realize.

Evolving measurable parameters

When it comes to evolving measurable parameters, the first thing that comes to my mind is the need to have a clear vision, objectives, well-defined and time-bound (both short term and long term) goals to reach the former within a specific time slot and a professionally prepared budget. Only against this we can measure the success or failure of our publications and products.

Our goals should not be too lofty and vague, but sustainable, stable, and easily measurable. Our policies should not easily change with the change of an editor or an administrator. I've seen this happening to many Catholic publications and the results have been disastrous.

With our objectives and goals clearly established, I feel that we should more often sit down to evaluate our performances. It is very desirable that the readers of our publications and the recipients of our products are also involved in this process of evaluation by means of questionnaires and feedback. I believe this is a surer way of assessing the success or failure of a publication.

As one who has edited a fairly popular national youth magazine, for over a decade, I am inclined to say that if we're able to take the major part of our target readership along with us, as we move on with our well-defined goals and objectives, we are definitely on the way to success, even though we may still be struggling to be financially viable, in spite of the fact that financial viability is highly desirable.

[Fr Alphonse Elengikal, ssp, belongs to the Congregation of the Society of St. Paul. He is the Editor of the popular national youth magazine, The Teenager.]

•••

4.3

THE MISSION AND VISION OF A CHURCH-RUN SECULAR PUBLICATION

Fr Xavier Vadakkekara, ofm. cap

I would like to begin with the narration of an Incident. Catholic nuns were raped in Gajruala in 1990. The Sunday Observer weekly from New Delhi broke the story 14 days after the act of rape. A Church news service in Delhi got the story two days after the event (that is 12 days before Sunday Observer broke it) but chose to ignore it. After Christians started protest marches for the cause of the nuns, and media launched campaigns in New Delhi and elsewhere, the news service carried a number of stories, but diligently avoided the word "rape."

Another incident which took place in 1997 - when a Catholic priest was falsely accused, stripped and paraded naked. Indian Currents was the first to bring out this human right violation and it supported it all through.

The mission of Catholic Media

All things Catholic should have only one mission. It emerges form the lucid and unambiguous Commission that Christ established - Go ye and preach to the world. Anything the Church do should either be ancillary to this mission or directly lead to this mission. Therefore, the mission of a Catholic-run secular publication should not be anything other than adhering to the Commission.

Church and secularism is a contradiction in terms. The moment Church becomes secular it ceases to exist. This is true either way we look at secularism - whether it is acceptance of all religions equally or negation of all of them considering the world as the only reality.

If Church cannot become secular, how far its activity could become secular? Let us avoid philosophy and theology and their attached escapist arguments. From the base level experience of over 25 years, I must say Church's scope to run a purely secular publication is decidedly limited. In other words, a Church publication has pronounced limitations in adapting the methods of profit-driven secular publications.

Then why does the Church need "secular-looking non-Churchy" publications? When the Capuchins took over the publication of Indian Currents, as a delegate of our congregation, I had long and enriching conversations with its founder editor Father John Vallamattam. He told me the primary aim of the publication was to "reach the Christian mind to the socio-political leadership of India." That I believe is the mission of a "non-Churchy" publication.

Let me make this mission a bit clearer lest I may be misunderstood. The mission of a secular-looking Church publication is not preaching the gospel directly. The publication is also not meant for running advocacy campaigns to create an atmosphere conducive for preaching the gospel. The mission, for me, is simply to inform its readers the "Christian mind" on events and opinions unfolded in the nations. It is to help reader form conclusions in the light of Christian ethics and values and thus should aid the establishment of the "Kingdom of God" as enunciated in the Gospels.

The "Christian mind," you would agree, may not be necessarily the mind of the hierarchy alone; and the Christian values would not contradict natural justice and human values.

Vision

A publication's vision naturally derives from its mission. I have certain vision about our readers, content and the management. I would like to reiterate here that the vision I enumerate are my own, and it does not relate in any way to any individual or organization.

Readers

A Church publication, if it wants to be secular despite its limitations, should cater to a wider audience. In other words, it should stop seeing the Church people as its sole readers. And therefore, it should not be a paper for self-glorification and pontification. At Indian Currents, we already look at all English-reading Indians as our readers.

Content

The liberative content of a Kingdom oriented publication

should naturally counter injustice, violence and moral degradation at all levels. For, it is our Baptismal mandate to fight satanic actions. Unfortunately, Church in India as a whole forgets to react adequately to such injustices in time.

Management

The management of Church-run publication should have the freedom of management -both financially and socially. The editor should have the freedom to choose the content. To that end, the publication should become financially independent.

The vision about a Church-run publication is still a dream. I would like to tell something about the challenges that block the growth potential of every Church run publication in India.

The Challenges

The reality of the Church

The Church in India is apparently more an idea today than a reality. Where is the Indian Church? We have dioceses, congregations, rites and regions vying with each other with varied self-motivated interests that we often tend to forget the great Commission of Christ. Since "Indian Church's" publications are owned and managed by varied interest groups we are yet to have a publication supported by the Indian Church.

To end this, a Church leadership needs to come up, that would have some say on the Church in India. Our formation should orient toward forming a hierarchy that would give utmost importance to the Word of God than anything else. With regret we understand so many of the high sounding resolutions passed by the CBCI and CRI over the past several decades are yet to be even read by our clergy and members of the congregations! This pathetic situation should end.

The reality of resources

Media need money, and Church media need Church's money. So far the Indian Church has not collectively decided to spend some money on some sort of media. Unfortunately, Christianity that started the printing press in India is still at experimental levels with print media. We need to give some serious thought on having an Indian Christian publication.

Reaching the higher echelons

A churchy publication does not make inroads into the political and governmental system. Indian Currents is a magazine being keenly watched by parliamentarians, judiciary, legislature and the media. It may be apt to point out here that an exclusive interview carried by Indian Currents with Mr. J.M. Lyngdoh, the then election commissioner at a time when he was putting his foot down on the timing of Andhra elections and not willing to meet the press, was taken up by Press Trust Of India (PTI) and was widely quoted by Times Of India and other leading publications.

One of the issues taken up and campaigned by Indian Currents is the case of migrant domestic workers from tribal states of Jharkhand and Chattisgarh being included in the central Unorganised Sector Workers - Protection Bill. The campaign has borne fruits with the government planning to incorporate these workers into the proposed bill.

Media ignorant hierarchy

There is much more in Media activities than publishing a newsletter or an audio-video cassette and this alone would not make one a media person. A minimum requirement of a media person is to read the daily newspaper or at least listen to news. Sadly, many in our hierarchy are too busy to spend sometime to know what is happening around the country and think a bit on why it is happening. I have heard bishops and major superiors mention that due to time constraints they are unable to read a daily newspaper or follow the news forget about Indian Currents.

Many think media is for self-glorification. Church people get easily offended when their personal interests are in some ways questioned in a media run by the Church. If a bishop has a problem with a congregation, the bishop would like to see the Church media projecting his views than what actually happened. Church people often forget that balanced professional reporting needs to project both sides. And they should not be offended if counter voices are heard in the media.

Media are not a emergency medical kit that would be pulled out and used in situations of rare personal needs. It should be seen as every day drinking water that sustains the life system of a society. We are yet to grow to have a grip on media. (Media is not for Gajraula alone—we should see Gajraula / Jhabua repeating every two minutes in India). As per statistics, there is a rape case every two minutes in India.

Truth challenges

Truth and justice become the biggest causality and challenge of the Church run media when they bewilder at actions of some people inside the Church. Could Church-run publications effectively challenge violence, injustice and moral degradation within the Church? If that is not possible, how could a Church run publication carry out its mission?

The Church as a community and organization has shortcomings. Captitation fees in a few institutions, unhealthy fights over rights of rites, financial mismanagement, increasing secularist tendencies among Church people are all facts. Can or will Church media ever take up its mission? Would the Church publication have the freedom to publish human rights violations against lay people such as denying Christian burial to a dead person?

Conclusion

Gajraula is symbolic. In a country like India no one can guarantee that such events would not be repeated. Let me repeat, what we need is not a medical kit to treat Gajruala, but water to drink so that we breath normal despite all sorts of such injustices and advances both within and outside the Church.

After speaking thus far, you might ask me why the Indian Currents couldn't become "the one publication" that would positively face the challenges. I would not dismiss that question as trash, but I would only ask you to learn about the basic realities, if you are serious about media. Media work needs men, money and time. The Capuchin congregation alone cannot make Church media in India!

I have seen the birth and death of at least half a dozen Catholic publications, some of them, dailies. It is worth making a study on why they died out, before making presumptions on the cause of their sad and sudden end.

A word of caution. I have seen media discussions happening within the Church for the past quarter of a century. The same old arguments are put forward to reach the same old resolutions that would be forgotten. Let us stop this and get into some action. A seminar a month would not make Church media in India, let us be sure of that.

[Fr Xavier Vadakkekara, ofm. cap., holds a Doctorate Degree in Mass Communications from the University of the Philippines. He is the editor-in-chief of Indian Currents weekly, the Director of Assisi Institute of Communications and Technology (AICT), which is affiliated to the Guru Jambeshwar University, Hisar, Haryana and the founding Director of Media House group of publications.]

•••

5

TRAINING IN COMMUNICATIONS

5.1

IS THE CHURCH IN INDIA MEDIA SAVVY?

Michael Gonsalves

How did a diocese in India handle an allègation of sexual abuse against a local pastor by an irrepressible lawyer accusing the cleric of molesting a 13-year-old girl? That the local press, including a national daily and some websites went to town "crucifying" the pastor without a "fair trial" is an understatement. The bishop, the CEO where the buck stops, willy-nilly bore the brunt.

Be that as it may, the mass media with inherent dog-eat-dog culture to get the news first and unearth the "hot" conflicting episode made the priest a villain and the advocate a hero for the days the issue was kept alive in the media and in the minds of the readers. The irreparable damage was down, even as more than the majority of the parishioners rallying behind the accused parish priest. Indeed, the reputation of the Church and clergy was sullied. For several days, the head honcho of the Church was dragged in the controversy.

Could the media blow have been a bit softer even as none could stop the hungry media newshounds for publishing the sensational news story to increase their circulation, their brand value, score over rivals, and satiate the appetite of the readers asking for more?

The answer is in the affirmative. If the diocese had a professional, trained journalist as its PRO, the church could have managed the situation honorably, just as most of the MNCs and other organizations do in the worst of times. The church, undoubtedly could have handled the press professionally. Unfortunately, as it happens in such cases, with the deadly combination of sex, religion and power, the fall out of the unsavory event was that it was not only the talk of the town among locals, the loose tongues began wagging everywhere, in the market place, in the place of work and what's more circulating unreported stories. This would not have come to pass or at least could have been contained, if the Church had a trained person to handle the crisis. The distilled ancient wisdom is we should not start digging a well when we are thirsty!

In fact, even as some agitated priests suggested to their superiors that the church version be sent to the 24-year-old Catholic news agency SAR (South Asian Religious) NEWS, the agency had already carried an on-the-spot analytical report, by one of its seasoned senior journalists, carrying the church version of the incident, the antecedents of the crusader of the event and the shenanigans of the mass media.

In a way, the report was more than a balancing act and told the reader the other side of the coin, to help him draw his own conclusions. But the bitter truth is that the diocese had not sent a statement to the Catholic news agency. That was the least it could do. But that is the ground reality not only of that diocese, but also of the more than majority of the dioceses in India. The hungry media needs to be fed not with a comprehensive statement but a preliminary statement as soon as whenever a scandal or a shocking incident breaks out of the Church or parish-run school or an institution. That is what any company or organization worth its salt in the face of a crisis does. And the church would do well if she follows suit, faced with such unfortunate sticky situations. A couple of newspapers carried the SAR NEWS agency report. The agency on its own did what it should do without fear or favor. It did what it did only because it is a Catholic agency run by Catholic journalists, with deep concerns for the affairs of the universal church.

Ever since for the first time printed Bibles began rolling out from the newly invented printing press of Johannes Gutenberg of Germany in the middle of the 15th Century, little did anyone dream or imagine the extraordinary and spectacular consequence this new communication technology would bring about, affecting every one on the face of this earth. The printing press increased both volumes and the speed of communication through books and newspapers. It began a print culture, huge in volume and reach, impacting thinking process and shaping public opinion. In Europe, the print culture competed and won over the preacher shouting in the street. Today we have been taken over by digital communication technologies, particularly the Internet and direct broadcast satellites. Since Gutenberg's time we have come a long. Today we are engulfed with an ever increasing news flow from the giant information superhighway, both in size, volume and reach.

With a rich legacy of having the first printing press at St Paul College in Goa during the Portuguese regime, the Church in India has not kept pace with the increasing demands from the media for information from within the church. We do not have adequate trained personnel to respond and issue rejoinders whenever the mass media maligns the reputation of the church. Or any organization through the use of the mass media throws a gauntlet at the church in general.

Journalism, as practiced in India may be literature in a hurry, and to be forgotten the next day, with the arrival of the day's fresh edition, carrying another big story, another scandal of the nation, but the wounds inflicted on the church take a long time to heal and a long time to regain the lost reputation from the people, especially of other faiths.

Archbishop John Foley, president of the Pontifical Council for Social Communications said the church does so many good works and there are so many good news stories, especially of building the community, building bridges between faiths, empowering the powerless, the voiceless, the marginalized and the oppressed. Many inspiring secular, developmental works carried out with unmatched devotion and dedication remain untold. Not that the church needs publicity but if told subtly in a professional way, it has the potential to earn the much-needed goodwill of the other community, of other faiths, especially in these hate-mongering times. And mould and shape the perception and opinion of the church favorably. These stories need to be told in the grammar and language of the media. The church needs a media vision and media mission not for one year but for the next 25 years with concrete budgetary allocations from its financial resources. The proverbial question is who will bell the cat.

If the church believes in the principles of professionalism and not in piecemeal approach, it is time to scout for talent in the laity, network, collaborate with the trained Christian and other sympathetic media experts, and trust and entrust them with not only freedom but with funds as well. The 40-year-old Indian Catholic Press Association, which runs the news agency, SAR News, will readily and willingly undertake consultancy work for the dioceses in India to build a professional, efficient, effective state-of-the-art social communication centers, with minimum investment to take care of all the media needs of the diocese.

Recognizing the greater power of the mass media to shape ideas and influence behavior, Pope John Paul II has said the media of social communications should be used to promote universal human values and thus, contribute to the renewal of society.

[The writer was formerly Editor of Pune Midday, Maharashtra Herald and The Free Press Journal. Currently, he is the President of Indian Catholic Press Association and Editor-in-Chief of SAR NEWS Agency.]

•••

5.2

AN ACTION PLAN TO SENSITIZE CHURCH LEADERS

Bishop Leo Cornelio, svd

The topic itself sounds far fetched at the first sight. An action plan to sensitize Bishops and Major Superiors! Well, they are supposed to be experts in 'everything', and of course, that includes communications as well! Nevertheless, the Final Statement of the CBCI GBM '04 clearly urges that "if a pastoral plan is to be successfully implemented, a proper formation programme should be arranged for all in the Church. All leaders of the community - bishops, priests, religious and lay leaders - should get adequate training in communications so that they can effectively discharge their duties for evangelization and defense of the genuine interests of the Church and society." (CBCI GBM '04, n. 17). Hence in the light of that mandate I wish share the following.

Fr. Henry D'Souza, our CBCI Executive Secretary for Communications, in his draft outline on 'Pastoral Plan For Social

Communications' has touched on most of the essential areas related to this subject and we have further discussed and elaborated on it.

Since the past decade or more, India has been experiencing 'media explosion' that has been impacting all aspects of human life. The vast expansion of human communication is profoundly influencing culture everywhere. In his Encyclical *Redemptoris Missio*, Pope John Paul II refers to the first '*Areopagus*' of modern age, that is, the world of communications, which as the Pope explains, "is the world of communications, which is unifying humanity and turning it into what is known as 'Global Village'. The means of social communications have become so important as to be for many the chief means of information and education, of guidance and inspiration in their behavior as individuals, families and within society at large. (RM, n. 37c)

The Church's stress on communications is rooted in a vision of communication as a way toward communion. It declared communication as "the giving of self in love" (*Communio et Progressio*, n. 11). In this respect communication mirrors the Church's own communion and capacity of contributing to it. We are convinced that along with traditional means or methods such as witness of life, catechesis, personal contacts, popular piety, liturgy and similar celebrations, the use of media is now very essential in evangelization and catechesis.

Pastoral Plan on the level of the diocese/ Local Church/ Province/ Region

It is now clear that serious effort is on in order to evolve a pastoral plan for social communication on the National, Regional and Diocesan levels. Such a pastoral plan is "to incarnate the prophetic, proclaiming mission of the Church in a media-shaped and media- conscious society" (FABC, BM '96). Here the responsibility of the bishops and Major Superiors cannot be overlooked.

On the occasion of FABC Plenary Assembly in Manila, January 1995, thc participants said in the final statement that the Asian Bishops "did not miss the value of the discovery of mass media for the promotion of values and support of people's movements and rights". At the same occasion Pope John Paul II reminded the Bishops that on them "rests the responsibility for fostering with wisdom and fidelity the most suitable means for communicating the Gospel to the various Asian cultures."

When we speak of communication training as such, it is something more or beyond the communication formation which is basic and essential for all (Cf. Church and Social Communication in Asia – 'Communication Formation in Asia by Fr. Franz-Josef Eilers, svd).

But such training in communication presupposes basic formation as a prerequisite. The FABC-OSC Bishops' Meet in 1997, discussing on the communication dimensions of a 'New way of being Church in Asia', sees the Church as a communion of communities, that is participatory, witnessing, dialoguing and prophetic. This would mean that communication formation has to be based on four specific dimensions, namely-

1. Community building
2. Encouraging co-responsibility at all levels
3. Witnessing and dialoguing, and
4. A prophetic sign

What kind of action plan for training in communication can be provided for Bishops and Major Superiors?

They being leaders of the Church, it is not easy to suggest a specific plan of action to train them. However, better skills and more training can– enhance their/ our efficiency and effectiveness. Some of the possible areas in which the Bishops and Major Superiors could be sensitized from time to time would be:

1. Seminars or workshops on Public Relations, relations between Church and Media, Crisis Management and training for public communication. The above areas should be the focus of such training (ref. Seminar BISCOM 1, 1 - Church and Public Relations). This area has become very important in our country in today's context.

2. Providing opportunities, through courses or seminars to experience/ know about the various modern means of communications available and being used at different levels and the ability to appreciate their effectiveness.

3. Develop sensitivity to the positive and negative effects of electronic media and modern means of communication on the society and the Church, especially on families and family values.

4. Building greater awareness about the use of traditional means of (Alternative Media) communication in evangelization even in the present age, such as – street plays, dramas, dances, popular songs and music etc.

5. Bishops and Major Superiors as heads of diocese/ religious communities should have/ learn the necessary skills to coordinate the communication personnel as well as apostolates. They should encourage collaboration on the level of the diocese/ ecclesiastical units and institutions owned and

administered by the religious congregations, namely – availability of personnel, sharing of technical expertise, equipment, avoiding duplication, competition, etc., in the media world.

The frequency of these seminars/ courses/ workshops could as per the needs of individual groups and their availability.

[Bishop Leo Cornelio, svd, is the Bishop of Khandwa diocese in central India. He has been the Provincial Superior of the Indore Province of the Society of the Divine Word and Assistant to the Superior General, Rome.]

...

5.3

TRAINING IN COMMUNICATION FOR PRIESTS, RELIGIOUS AND THOSE IN FORMATION

Bishop Chacko Thottumarickal, svd

Communication is a widely used term today and yet it means different things for different people. The simple act of communication is often mixed up with technologies of communication. While technologies may facilitate communication, in itself it need not be identified with technology. Therefore it is better to clarify the term before speaking about training in communication.

The Concept

Communication is often narrowly understood as the use of media and specially the use of modern mass media and electronic gadgets. Due to this narrow understanding, the scope of communication is often limited to some trained specialists. But the vistas of communications is very vast and includes such areas as verbal communication, non-verbal communication, interpersonal communication, intra-personal communication, body language, culture as communication, public relations and prayer as communication with God.

The remark that the communication people are often the least communicative is a pointer to the fact that communication experts themselves often limit the understanding of the concept to the media of communication. As social beings, humans have a need to communicate. The growth and health of individuals and societies depend a lot on their ability to communicate.

Real communication is between persons. It indicates a process of mutual giving and receiving. Ideally, it is a two way process. The media are expected to facilitate this process of communication and cannot become a substitute to the process. Just for an example, consider the marvel of mobile phones. People can keep in touch with each other anytime and anywhere. But possessing a mobile does not make one a communicating person, if one does not carry it with him and does not keep it switched on. If true communication takes place between persons, it leads to relatedness, sharing, collaboration, participation, co-operation and leads to communion.

The objective of communication training is to prepare a communicating generation and withstand the tendencies of isolated and exclusivist life. These two tendencies of the modern world which are gaining currency are a threat to communication.

Types of Training

One of the important areas which require training is interpersonal communication. Many problems in pastoral and religious life are due to a break down in this area. As social beings, we do communicate but often much more is expected but not delivered. This gap is due to ignorance of the blocks which are from within. Knowing oneself and one's blocks is very important. There are many counselling centres in the country which provide help to individuals as well as train people with helping skills. These courses help intra-personal and inter-personal communication. Those in formation whether as future priests or religious, need to be given this course as a part of the general curriculum. Those who require special attention should have extra time allotted to improve interpersonal communication. The orientation of openness and transparency should be developed. PRH centre in Bangalore conducts regularly courses in this area.

Another important area is Public relations. A priest and a religious perform many services for the society in which they live. They are not private persons. There is a growing awareness about this important area today. Many dioceses and institutions today have a PRO including CBCI. But much more is to be done so that it becomes an integral part of our life and activities. Although it is important for all, there are some who are naturally talented in this area. These persons should be identified and given specialised training and encouragement so that they can project the good face of the institutions and organizations. The training programmes given by persons like Mr. Allwyn Fernandes should be part of the formation in seminaries and religious life.

Crisis management is another area which we need to be prepared for. When we are taken by surprise, our communication often breaks down or are paralysed. Mock sessions and analysis of crisis situations which were handled in the past can be helpful to develop some skills in this area.

As far as the media of communication are concerned, two

areas which need attention are the production in media and the use of media. Media productions are capital intensive and need special skills. Training in journalism is feasible at the formation stages and later. Various aspects of production in radio, Television and cinema can be considered although may not be always practical to set up production centres. But we can train talented people to work in the commercial sector and public sector. Many institutes and universities today offer short and long courses in India. NISCORT in Delhi does a commendable job.

Another important area of training is to be in the area of consumption of media, which is commonly known as media education. There is a flooding of printed materials, television channels, radio stations and Cinema so that the common man is almost getting drowned in them. Through media education we can train the young and old to appreciate and selectively use media and evaluate the media content and message. With a lot of trash being produced, violence and vulgarity being available, enlightened consumption and discerned digestion is a need. Media education should be part of the curriculum of all formation houses and educational institutions. This training can be a part of the moral education class in schools. Teachers and formators need to be introduced to Media Education. Many regional centres are already doing it.

Folk media is very close to the life and culture of ordinary people. In rural India, folk media play an important role in communication. Training in music, dance, street theatre and other forms of folk arts add to the skills of priests and religious. Workshops can be arranged to demonstrate the power of this medium and impart skills.

Group media are influential as far as the message is

concerned. It is important for missionaries to be familiar with group media methodology, if the message of salvation is to be communicated effectively.

Duration

For the priests and religious short courses of two months/ one month/ one week could be organized at the diocesan and regional levels. For those in formation, many of the areas of communication can be integrated in a graded manner during the years of formation. Those who need greater specialization can go for degree and diploma courses conducted in the Universities and institutes.

Medium

The medium of training should pay importance to the vernacular languages. The ordinary man in India communicates in the vernacular. It has maximum effect. English is important due to its reach across the regions and nations but has its own limitations. Hence the regional languages should be given due importance.

Resource persons

We have many resource persons in the country who can provide training. An important need is to compile a database of such persons and keep it updated and available.

Media skills Training Centres

There are many institutions in India which offer short and long term training for those interested. Some of them are the following: NISCORT in Delhi, *Gurjarvani* in Ahmedabad, *Ishvani* in Pune, *Xavier Institute of communications* in Mumbai, *Amruthavani* in Secunderabad, *Yuva Prachodini* in Bangalore, Santhome in Chennai, Kalai Kaveri in Trichy, Satprakashan in Indore, Nav Chetana in Bhopal, *Ravi Bharati* in Patna, *Notre Dame* in Patna, *Nitika* in Kolkota, *Sandesha* in Mangalore and many universities and colleges. It is up to us to benefit from them and offer appropriate training to our personnel, so that they truly become 'Messengers of the New Age.'

[Bishop Chacko Thottumarickal is the first bishop of the recently created diocese of Jhabua in central India. He holds a masters degree in Mass Communications from the University of Leicester. Formerly he was the SVD Provincial Superior of the Indore Province.]

...

New Language, New Culture

"The world is seeing the emergence of a new culture that 'originates not just from whatever content is eventually expressed, but from the very fact that there exist new ways of communicating, with new languages, new techniques and a new psychology'. The exceptional role played by the means of social communication in shaping the world, its cultures and ways of thinking has led to rapid and far-reaching changes in Asian societies."

(Ecclesia in Asia n. 48)

5.4

PROFESSIONAL TRAINING FOR THE CHURCH AND MAINSTREAM MEDIA

Fr Sebasti L. Raj, sj

01. The Catholic Church considers it one of its duties to announce the Good News of salvation with the help of the media of social communication and to instruct men in their proper use. It is, therefore, "an inherent right of the Church to have at its disposal and to employ any of these media insofar as they are necessary or useful for the instruction of Christians and all its efforts for the welfare of souls" (*Inter Mirifica,* n. 3).

02. Further, *Communio et Progressio* declares that the new skills and techniques of communication "serve to build new relationships and to fashion a new language which permits men to know themselves better and to understand one another more easily. By this, men are led to a mutual understanding and shared ambition.... The tools of communication, then, provide some of the

most effective means for the cultivation of that charity among men which is at once the cause and the expression of fellowship" (*Communio et Progressio,* n. 12).

03. The same document is particular that one should "have a full and proper understanding of man. He must also have a sound knowledge both of the true nature of social communication and of the tools at its service" (n. 15). According to this document, if the media of social communication are to give their best service to mankind, the importance of the human element must be recognized. This element plays a more decisive role than the most marvellous electronic and mechanical instruments by themselves. It further says that "both communicators and recipients ... need a suitable grounding if full advantage is to be taken of the opportunities offered by these instruments" (n. 63).

04. *Communio et Progressio* is very clear about the need for professional training in the field of social communications. It says: "Many communicators handle well the tools of their profession, but lack a deep understanding of the art of communicating with all it implies. It is obvious that the communicators in the media who wish to excel, need a serious and specialized training in every aspect of their work. The growing trend to found faculties of social communication in institutions of higher learning is a welcome development" (n. 71). This document makes a comparison between the apostles and their time and our time and underlines the need to make proper and full use of the modern means of communication, which cannot be done unless one is professionally qualified. It goes to the extend of stating: "Indeed it would be difficult to suggest that Christ's command was being obeyed unless all the opportunities offered by the modern media to extend to vast numbers of people the announcement of his Good News were being used" (n. 126).

05. In another place, the same document says that "every effort should be made to use the most appropriate technique and style in fitting a communication to its medium". It also underlines the fact that "the latest media of social communication are indispensable means for evangelization, and enlightening the minds and heart of men". This can be done only by those who are specialized professionally. The above document acknowledges this fact and states that "trained and experienced men must be found for this work". Further, it declares that the official Catholic organizations and enterprises that work in social communications with a pastoral end in view should be able to call upon trained personnel. Hence, the training of laymen, priests and religious is to be given a high priority by those responsible for this work in the Church." (n. 131, 163, 162,164, 170).

06. *Inter Mirifica* wants to establish Catholic press, radio stations and television channels. In today's world of high competition and crisis of values, it is impossible to run a successful media centre, unless there are highly qualified and capable persons, with a lot of creative ideas and technical capabilities (n. 14). Hence, it declares that "priests, religious and laymen who are equipped with the proper skills for adapting these media to the objectives of the apostolate should be appointed promptly. Importantly, laymen ought to be afforded technical, doctrinal and moral training." (n. 15).

07. Speaking about the formation of priests and pastoral workers, *Aetatis Navae* reiterates the need to train them appropriately in the field of social communications and says: "Education and training in communications should be an integral part of the formation of pastoral workers and priests.... They must ... be prepared to minister both to the 'information-rich' and to the 'information-poor'.... As for those who will be actively engaged in media work for the Church, they need to acquire professional skills in media along with

doctrinal and spiritual formation" (n. 18). Further, this document is very particular that the "strategies in the field of social communications must be based on the results of sound media research which have been subjected to informed analysis and evaluation" (n. 32). This implies highly qualified professionals so that they are able to undertake such research programmes.

08. Concrete Proposals

In the light of the above reflections on the teaching of the Church, the following proposals can be offered for consideration:

8.1 This is an era of specialization and hence the Church cannot be effective if its members are not professionally qualified for any of its ministries. This is all the more true of the field of social communications, since it involves highly technical knowledge and capability. In order to prepare effective professionals, the Church should allot personnel and funds for specialized studies. Short courses, introductory courses, self-taught knowledge of the media, etc. will not suffice to meet today's demands. The Church has to think and act professionally in order to be effective in this world, which has adopted a highly professional way of behaviour and functioning.

8.2 Since social communications is basically a tool to be used in all the ministries of the Church, it is not enough just to train one or two persons in a diocese and imagine that it would suffice for effective ministries. We have to train everyone who is in charge of different ministries or are holding important responsibilities, since effective communication is the requirement in all aspects of the Church – formation, pastoral care of the Catholics, evangelization of the people of other faiths, administration, public relations, etc.

8.3 In order to be professionally effective, our training has to be as close to the culture and background of the people as possible. This implies that a merely theoretical specialization which is far removed from the location and culture of the place of our ministries will be of little use and effect. In other words, the training should be as much contextualized as possible, while being technically professional.

8.4 We need to encourage institutes of higher studies and research centres to engage in both applied and fundamental research related to communication needs and concerns of the Church and society.

8.5 We need to support ongoing theological reflection upon the processes and instruments of social communications and their role in the Church and society.

[Fr. Sebasti L. Raj, SJ, is presently the Director of NISCORT. He has been the Director of the Indian Social Institute for many years and has undertaken a number of surveys and evaluation projects of national importance.]

...

5.5

TRAINING OF LAY PEOPLE IN COMMUNICATIONS

K.M. Selvaraj

Let me place on record, the wonderful work undertaken by the CBCI Commission for Social Communications for preparing the Pastoral Plan for Social Communications and for its dedication to implement the same with earnestness.

Some of the communalist forces in India are much concerned, about the way the communication is spread by the Catholic Church to every part of the globe. Believe me I am not flattering you, they envy the Church's organizational set up. Thanks to the effective networking of Union of Catholic Asian News - UCAN correspondents in India, are disseminating the information to the Western world swiftly. Within the country, the services of South Asian Religious News - SAR News is commendable. Through these agencies - news of attacks on the minority institutions and Church personnel reach faster to the publication houses.

Being the editor of a secular newspaper in the Ootacamund diocese, I have been invited to every Press Conference by the local Member of Parliament belonging to the then ruling party. It gives me an opportunity to learn how some of the communal organizations operate. Their way of enrolling the youth to spread their ideology from the grassroots level is amazing. They have already established their units in the remote villages of our country - you know the method they use is through Mass Media, they have faithful reporters and workers in every media across the country.

Problems of a country like India are many and there is the need for planning and looking for solutions at the macro and grassroots levels. The media have a very important role to play in this process of development for all. The media can help to create awareness and empower people. Unless the Church wakes up to the urgency of Social Communications and trains the Laity in the field of Mass Media, we will be left behind to face threats and challenges. It is a discouraging fact that even now quite a number of dioceses do not have a proper pastoral plan and those who have one, have not yet integrated media ministry into it.

Vatican II stresses the role of the laity in the mission of the Church. Accordingly, there has been a steady increase of laity participation in the various ministries of the Church. In many dioceses the Basic Christian Communities, Parish Councils, Pious Associations and the diocesan Pastoral Councils provide ample scope for the participation in the mission of the Church. Training of Laity in and for media work can be fulfilled to a large extent if the local churches have a positive outlook and are ready to support them financially as well. This is important because training in the mass media is rather expensive.

Church authorities may have the apprehension that once trained, the Laity may rather seek jobs in the secular media than support the Church media centres. This may discourage them from supporting the training of laity. In fact there are training media centres where talented young laypersons are kept under trained and under paid. Instead, the Church should take up the challenge of training talented young persons to pursue career in the secular media. Getting lay personnel into the secular media is one of the major ways to evangelize the secular media as asserted in *Redemptoris Missio*.

Public Relations

Public Relations is a recent thrust in the Indian Church. It came in almost as response to the various atrocities on Church Personnel by the fanatic communal forces. Some might express surprise at this sudden interest of the Church in Public Relations which is basically an image building exercise keenly practiced by companies and firms to promote sales and foster goodwill. "For effective relationships the Church needs to integrate public relations and communication training among the Church personnel at all levels." This should start with the training of seminarians and lay people committed to the Church. For PR in the Church it is desirable to have knowledgeable and committed laymen / women as Public Relations officers, with a well - defined job description. The PR office should be well equipped with documentation and data bank. There should also be sufficient communication facilities like phone, fax, E-mail, Internet etc., to collect and supply information to the public before the public gets the distorted version from elsewhere. This should be a permanent office, not a mere crisis management cell. The PR should be part of the pastoral plan of the diocese or the Episcopal region and financially supported by the Church.

Action Plan

1) The Church should be able to invest more in the training of the laity. They could be given foundational courses in Theology, Catechetics and Bible so that they have sound Christian formation.

2) The laypersons who have established themselves in the secular media on their own, should be encouraged, supported and appreciated. Church media personnel need to help them with means for their animation and updating not only the technical fields, but also in Theological and ethical areas.

3) The Laity needs to be included in the decision - making process of the media centres. Often it is seen that they are given secondary roles while priests and religious occupy important positions under the pretext of cheap labour and greater availability. This leads to non-professionalism and lack of accountability.

4) The clergy working in the Church media centres should take special interest to give opportunities of internship to lay persons in Church media centres, further even help them to secure a placement in the secular media.

5) Each Catholic educational institution should have a PRO and highlight the achievements of the students who have secured high marks in the public exams, won prizes in the sports and other extra curricular activities. Talents for communications should be identified and encouraged already from the school level.

6) Media Education should be made compulsory for students in our institutions. Regular Letters to the Editor, Film Review, Debate on TV Serials, News Analysis classes will make the students media savvy. Students should be exposed to the world of Internet. A core group comprising teachers and students should be entrusted with the task of writing the press releases and get them published through the local media.

7) Extensive opportunities are available with the electronic media, especially through the Cable TV network. Laity could be encouraged to produce programmes and get them telecast over

these networks. As per the principle of the survival of the fittest, in the media market, experience will make the lay technicians and producers become masters in the course of time.

8) Train the Trainers - through the diocesan communication centres. Once in 6 months regular vicariate level workshops to be conducted for select lay leaders in turn they should be encouraged to disseminate the knowledge to their members in the parishes. The subjects could be Family Relations, Human and Legal Rights, Consumer Awareness, Eco Preservation, Governments Policies and Programmes, Political Awareness, Globalization and so on.

9) The resources of the Church should be made available to the laity to have training not only within the country but also if need be in the Western countries too. If each diocese has at least 5 lay resource persons to teach media education, we can be rest assured that we will have a vibrant communicating Church really. With the enthusiasm now seen among the Church leaders, I am confident the day is not too far, I once again thank the CBCI Commission for Social Communications for the wonderful opportunity to share my thoughts.

[Mr. K. M. Selvaraj is presently Secretary of the Indian Catholic Press Association and Editor, Nilgiris Today a secular bilingual weekly, Editor of Jokes, Quotes and Tit Bits Journal English Fortnightly and Tamil Catholic Laity Monthly Magazine in Tamil.]

Bibliography:

a) Babel to Babri Masjid and Beyond by Fr. Jacob Srambical, sj and Leela Joseph
b) UNESCO Publication
c) Media Education by Fr. Peter Gonsalves, sdb
d) Vatican II
e) Redemptoris Missio

•••

5.6

LEVERAGING MEDIA INTERACTION INTO AN OPPORTUNITY

Allwyn Fernandes

Media interaction is an opportunity to clarify doubts and communicate one's key messages. One can turn the challenging media interview into an occasion to shed light on relevant issues. How?

I. Pre-Interview Checklist

Before one starts the interview, it would be helpful to follow this checklist.

1. Name of interviewer : ______________________
2. From (name of media) : ______________________
3. Purpose of interview : ______________________
4. Date/time of interview : ______________________

5. Location of interview : ____________________

6. Have you read recent articles or seen/heard recent clips of broadcasts by this person?

Headline 1 : ____________________

Headline 2 : ____________________

7. How would you expect this person's attitude to be towards you in this interview?

Friendly [ ] Neutral [ ] Unfriendly [ ] Confrontational [ ]

8. Who will listen to/read/see this interview? :

9. Describe their probable attitudes? :

10. Your key message # 1 : ____________________

Fact : ____________________

Your key message # 2 : ____________________

Fact : ____________________

Your key message # 3 : ____________________

Fact : ____________________

11. Likely Questions and Answers:

Q : ____________________

A : ____________________

II. Important tips

Don't go by:

- Media's definition/ understanding/perspective of problem.
- Redefine it positively, the way Church sees it.

1. "The Church's key objective is the education of the poor and their empowerment...This is our core commitment. Therefore, when we heard of..."

Bridging Phrases:

- "Let me put that in perspective..."
- "What's really important to remember is ..."
- "That's not my area of expertise, but what I can tell you is..."
- "That's an important point because ..."
- "Let me just add..."
- "That's a good point, but what is equally important is ..."
- "What it all boils down to is..."
- "The point I wish to emphasise is..."

Turning Negatives into Positives:

- "Yes, but look at this..."
- "What I can confirm at this time is…"
- "What people need to know is that…"
- "In order to put that into perspective, we need to talk about…"
- "It is important to remember that…"
- "What I can tell you right now is…"
- "I don't have those details at this time, but I will find out and get back to you by...If I can please have your number…"

Answering Persistent Questions:

Q: How could you let this happen?
A: "The cause of this incident is unknown at this time; however, we will leave no stone unturned until we find out exactly what happened."

Q: Was it incompetence or stupidity that caused this?
A: "Probably neither. But let's wait for the report of the inquiry."

Q: Your institution went through a similar crisis/incident last year. Didn't you learn anything from that situation?
A: "We will not know who or what caused this incident till the

investigation has been completed. We cannot draw any conclusions until we fully understand every possible aspect of the situation."

Learn how to:

- Be proactive.
- Handle crisis communications with media.
- Manage public expectations at the outset.
- Build an initial response team.
- Prepare stand-by tools.
- Get ahead of the damage curve.

Try to acquire:

- Assessing risks.
- Consultation strategies.
- Crisis planning tools.

Learn how to

- Prepare for/negotiate interviews.
- Define and structure your news message.
- Use bridging phrases.
- Skilfully employ quotes and sound bites.
- Troubleshoot difficult questions.
- Handle verbal and non-verbal communication.

"God, give us Men! A time like this demand
Strong Minds, great hearts, true faith and ready hands,
Men who possess opinions and a will
Tall men, Sun-crowned who live above the fog
In public duty and in private thinking".

[Mr. Allwyn Fernandes is a professional journalist. At present he is the Vice President of R&P Management Communications Pvt. Ltd., Mumbai. He has been a much appreciated resource person at the FABC and CBCI level animation programmes.]

...

Catholic Instruments of Communications

"Along with its other commitments in the area of communications and media, the church must continue, in spite of the many difficulties involved, to develop, maintain, and foster its own specifically catholic instruments and programmes of communications. These include the Catholic press and Catholic publishing houses, Catholic radio and television, offices of public information and media relations, institutes and programmes for training in and about media, research, and Church related organizations of communications professionals."

(Aetatis Novae, n. 17)

6

IMPROVING COORDINATION, NETWORKING AND ACCOUNTABILITY

6.1

COORDINATION OF COMMUNICATIONS ACTIVITIES AT REGIONAL / DIOCESAN LEVEL

Fr Cedric Prakash, sj

Introduction

The Proposed National Pastoral Plan for Social Communications (NPPSC) lays emphasis for a coordinated effort for communications and media related activities at the diocesan and regional levels.

I sincerely think that there can be no two opinions about this. For a Pastoral Plan to be effective and in fact implementable, there must be a coordinated effort at every possible level. In this short presentation, let me put forth the reality, some of my concerns and some suggestions on what we should be doing.

The Reality

Most of us are aware of the reality. This reality, though in many ways integrated, can broadly be categorized into three areas:

(a) **Our Media Centres:** In most of the dioceses, we have several Media Centres and all of us are doing plenty of communication / media activities. If we look at the Western Region, we have excellent work being done by Centres like the Pauline Communications, Xavier Institute of Communications, the Centres run by Salesians, The *Gujarat Sahitya Prakash* in Anand, to name just a few. Each of these Centres has been doing what it does either because of a particular charism of the congregation or of a specific need from time to time. Most of them are highly professional with a tremendous outreach and catering to diverse needs of people and in particular the Catholic / Christian community. In this category would also belong the weekly / monthly magazines and other bulletins brought out by the Dioceses or by specific institutions.

(b) **Our Spokes-persons / Communicators:** These are persons and / or institutions that speak on behalf of the Church and very especially when some interventions are needed. These either emerge because of their involvements in particular situations or because they have been appointed to act on behalf of the institution or the diocese.

(c) **The Diaspora:** This in a way constitutes the bulk of communication / media activities within a diocese or a region. Very often it is because of gifted or charismatic individuals that such activities take place: street-plays, puppet- shows, songs, dance, drawing / painting, cartooning, writing and the whole gamut of alternative media. This sphere belongs not merely to the clergy and religious within the Church structure, but also very much to the laity because quite often it also becomes their livelihood.

This, in a very simplistic way, is how I would like to paint the reality of communications / media activities in a diocese and in fact, a region. This obviously leads us to the second dimension namely concerns which arise from this reality.

The Concerns

The concerns are several but I would like to highlight just a few of them:

(i) There is a tremendous lack of communication among the so called "communicators" within a diocese or regional set-up.

(ii) There is practically no coordination at any level. Each one / centre does their own thing.

(iii) In most dioceses, the bishops have failed to understand the need and importance of communications / media activities and have not appointed the necessary personnel to help in the coordination of these activities.

(iv) There is a tendency of one-up-man-ship and we-are-better-than thou attitude especially when it comes to those Centres which have the complete backing of their religious congregation.

(v) There has been no effort being made either to establish Diocesan Commissions for Social Communication or for that matter Regional ones.

(vi) Coordination is sometimes interpreted as "control" and therefore many do not want to get into this trap.

(vii) Most often, the Church does not provide the necessary space for critical thinking whether it is of government structures or even the Church structures.

Suggestions

At this juncture, I would like to make two very concrete suggestions in the context of the concerns I have just mentioned:

1. Let the Church have the political will to ensure that this National Pastoral Plan for Social Communications is implemented by every single diocese all over the country.

2. This NPPSC cannot be implemented if there is no data-base of those involved with communications or media activities in a diocese or region.

Only when this above is in place, will we have a coordinated and cohesive effort for our plans and programmes.

Conclusion

What I presented here is a very skeletal outline of the need and importance of coordination at the diocesan and regional levels. So many of us have been caught up in mere words. It is high time that we start putting words into concrete action. Only then can we consider ourselves "communicators" moving towards excellence and in the footstep of the "Master Communicator - Jesus"

[Fr. Cedric Prakash, s.j. is a Human Rights activist and the Director of PRASHANT, the Jesuit Centre of Human Rights, Justice and Peace in Gujarat. He is also the Secretary of the Commission for Social Communications of the Western Region Catholic Bishops' Council.]

•••

6.2

IMPROVING COORDINATION, NETWORKING AND ACCOUNTABILITY

Fr Dominic Emmanuel, svd

Introduction

- What is networking?
  - Website comes from Cobweb, Net and Internet!
- Where could networking be useful?
- The post-modern world, as our current world and age is often described, is an inter-disciplinary age. No area of life is fully self-sufficient and there are no grand theories to explain various phenomena in the world. They are all inter-dependent.
- Networking can be among people of same interests or with varied interests. Networking, in our context, with all the media people would fall under the first category i.e. people

of the same interest. But media people networking for instance with human right activists or social workers or educationists would be networking with people of varied interests.

Why is networking required?

- For pooling of resources, of ideas, experiences, physical labour etc.
- Coordination means – Harmonization, synchronization, organization.
- Now networking necessarily means coordination but coordination does not necessarily always mean cooperation.
- Networking and coordination are more of a technical process whereas in cooperation human element plays a major role to achieve desired results.

Cooperation

- Cooperation could have been a concept that could have been added here or replaced more usefully with coordination. Cooperation is one area that desperately needs to be looked into within the Church and its personnel. We are all dedicated men and women working for a single cause and yet we find it so hard when it comes to cooperation among ourselves. Individual egos, bickering, pulling each other down destroy so much of our creative energies.

Accountability

- That brings me to the point of accountability. It is not enough for us to make sweeping statements about lack of cooperation and complete absence of accountability amongst our personnel.

- Accountability, though primarily connected with accounts of what you have in terms of income and expenditure and should be measured according to one's investment against the dividend one receives.
- In our context we need to see what investment has been made in projects, in training personnel for a specific job and compare that to the outcome in terms of impact or influence we have made on public and society. A similar principle must be applied to individuals in the Church.
- There has been a huge debate in the recent times on labour laws and the need to reform them. One of the things, for good or for bad brought in by globalisation is the rule of 'hire and fire'. In private firms if one cannot be accountable for his/her responsibility and does not perform as expected, he/she is immediately demoted or fired. One is therefore bound to perform, something that the Church personnel should learn greatly from.
- But accountability should really begin by asking as to what we have put up, such as buildings, studios, equipments and so on, was really necessary. Was it well thought out and planned? Jeevan TV is one example. Several of our projects stand like white elephants.
- Accountability is connected closely with professionalism, which is often completely absent from many of the Church organizations in general and media offices in particular.
- Responsibility is nearly the same as accountability and no networking is possible if people are not responsible or accountable.

Suggestions for Networking

- Diocesan Media offices around the country should be connected up.
- A Press release in one city should be made known and available immediately through networking in other cities too for publication.
- Simiiarly any news or happening or event should be immediately shared with all.
- Networking with our Christian news agencies such as UCAN, SAR, Fides, Zenit, Vatican Information Service and so on.
- Networking with Catholic publications such as The Examiner, Indian Currents, New Leader, The Herald, Voice of Delhi and many other diocesan publications.
- Networking with radio stations such as Radio Veritas, Radio Vatican or even Television channels.

There is a thin line dividing networking and keeping contacts with secular media in a place. Not everything that happens would interest secular media therefore there may not be a need to keep them informed about every single event.

[Rev. Dr Dominic Emmanuel, svd, is presently the Spokesperson and Director of the Communication/Information Bureau of the Delhi Catholic Archdiocese. He is the President of Signis India and has been involved in broadcasting over Radio Veritas Asia and Jain TV Channel. He has to his credit nearly 200 articles in the national dailies in Hindi and English.]

...

6.3

COORDINATION OF COMMUNICATIONS ACTIVITIES IN TAMIL NADU

Fr Vincent Chinnadurai

The Region of Tamil Nadu has 17 dioceses. All the dioceses have commissions for communication. Major religious congregations including some women religious orders have media and communication offices. Some, institutes of higher learning in Tamil Nadu run by Christians, have made media and communication, an integral part of their mission of Education. To cap it all, we have a fairly well manned and equipped Regional Coordinating Centre – that is Santhome Communications Centre, which has a history of 28 years. In the last two years Signis too is becoming robust and active in our region. It is generally agreed that the Church of Tamil Nadu has been effective and pro-active in the field of social communication and we even hear several Christian names in the mainline media industry and communication.

In brief I can state with satisfaction that in terms of human potential, micro and macro level structures for delivery – the region of Tamil Nadu is very well placed in the area of synergising the potentials and efficient coordination and networking between the various structures of social communication within the church. Under the able guidance and leadership of our Chairman, Bishop Antony Devotta we have resolved to vigorously work on these two areas – for added emphasis, I repeat – synergizing the potentials and effective coordination.

It may also be appropriate to state here that our involvement in the mission of social communication has the following dimensions:

- Evangelization
- Catechesis and other pastoral needs
- Human development with emphasis on information, education, civil society and social justice
- Politics of inclusion and democracy as opposed to communalism and neo-fascism

Keeping these in focus, we have evolved an action plan titled **"MISSION 2020"**. This draft plan was presented to the TNBC by the Chairman Bishop and the entire Council enthusiastically endorsed the vision.

The major elements of this road map for the next 16 years are:

- Equipping fully all the diocesan communications offices with personnel, structures and equipment to assist the entire Church of Tamil Nadu in the mission of evangelization and catechesis.
- To become a significant player in Tamil Nadu in shaping public opinion and social behaviour through mass media.

- Establish a FM/AM Catholic Radio Station (assuming that future laws will permit it) for every diocese, so that all the diocesan priorities/activities can be coordinated through the Radio. Bishops will address their faithful regularly. Catechism teachers will be equipped through the radio. Fund raising for social welfare projects can be coordinated through the radio. There will a dynamic relationship between the Basic Christian Communities and this Radio. The Radio will give operational inputs to the Basic Christian Communities. With such participation there will be an unleashing of the human talents and potentials.
- Connect all the diocesan centres, parishes, schools and other institutions with Internet connectivity through one satellite transponder, so that communication between various organs of the Church would become effective and cheaper.
- An institute excellence will be established by the year 2010 for media training.
- Adopt 1000 villages for Internet literacy by the year 2010.

In the immediate context, we have already set in motion two major initiatives through which we are attempting to bring all the major structures of social communications within the regional church. In these efforts the structure would also include major seminaries and colleges. The first one is known as SEARCH and second one is a 24 hours web-Satellite Radio Broadcasting.

SEARCH Programme

Church has the historic tradition of nurturing the talents and capabilities of its members. In fact in every parish celebration, in every school event we see celebration of talents. However one intriguing aspect is the gross under representation of our talents in the mainstream media and society. A careful and closer scrutiny would point to some valuable indicators.

1. Though our Children and youth are generally talented and though we identify them at the Parish-vicariate-diocesan levels, there has been no effort so far to identify the best, sharpen their talents with further training and make them powerful communicators and performers.
2. There is no stable and effective mechanism available within the Church to effectively link our talents with the mainstream media and society.

Taking all these factors in to consideration, Santhome Communications Centre intends to come out with a robust plan to search, identify, and train our young talents for the mission of communication. This important initiative will be known as "SEARCH". The search will begin at the parish level and celebrated at the regional level. The proactive cooperation and support of the Bishops, Communication Directors, Youth Commission and various diocesan units as well as the participation of the Religious is very important for the success of this very important mission. We earnestly begin the "SEARCH" from August 20.

Ulaga(th) Thamizh Osai

On the occasion of the assembly of bishops in Ooty in July 2004, Santhome Communications Centre launched the 24 hours web based radio- Ulaga(th) Thamizh Osai. Tamils all over the world can get access to this meaningful broadcast through our worldwide web **www.intamil24.com**. Proper news, family based programmes, Bible based dramas, inter-religious programmes, educative-innovative programmes, spiritual programmes, good interviews, meaningful debates, and refreshing songs will form the general content input.

Launching of this web-radio is only a preparatory stage for more ambitious expansion efforts in the near future.

By December 2004, we hope to expand this broadcast via satellite so that Tamil speaking expatriates in USA, Canada and Europe can listen to our programmes through their home-installed radio.

And we look forward to the day when the new Govt. will further liberalize FM broadcasting in India and drastically reduce the license premium. As and when this happens, Santhome will remain ready to make the courageous plunge to start FM/AM broadcastings.

Conclusion

We believe action brings people, resources and structures together. It is through these concrete activities we intend to make coordination and networking effective in our region.

[Presently Fr. Vincent Chinnadurai is the Regional Secretary of the TNBC Commission for Social Communications and Director of Santhome Communications Centre, Chennai. He is also Public Relations Officer of the Regional Bishops' Council and former editor of the Tamil Magazine, Namvazhu.]

...

6.4

PARISH COMMUNICATION COMMITTEE (PCC)

Fr Arun Ignatius Abraham, sj

Whether in the rural remotes or in the urban settings, practically every Parish/ Mission Station has access to a TV set, a Video or CD player, and a PA system. Most of the time they are the Parish Priests who, out of their busy schedules, take out time to organize some parish level audiovisual shows or other media presentations, either for formation / education or entertainment purposes. Ordinarily, such exercises remain quite limited as they depend mostly on the free time of the Parish Priests and their interests. Also, the transfers of the Parish Priests often affect the continuity of such exercises, adversely.

In the light of the above it is proposed that a committee of 5-7 selected laypersons is constituted in each of the Parishes/ Mission Stations and the responsibility of organizing Parish-level communication related activities is handed over to it. This Committee may be called the **Parish Communication Committee *(PCC)***.

The **PCC** will normally consist of the Secretary of the Parish Council, one representative each from the Youth, Women and Basic Christian Community (BCC) Wings of the Parish, and 2 – 3 persons who are selected/ nominated by the Parish Council on the basis of their talents/ interests.

The **PCC,** a voluntary Committee, constituted out of the interested/ selected lay Parishioners, will primarily be an active link between the Parish and the Diocesan Communication Commission/ Secretary. It shall function under the guidance of the Parish Council, and its sole objective would be to provide communication support to the Parish life.

The **PCC** once organized, will not only ensure the continuity of the communication media related activities organized at the Parish-level, it can also provide communication support to different apostolic wings of the Parish.

Most of the times, the Parishes are the points of reference when it comes to carrying out of any communication related project pertaining to the faithful. Formation of the ***PCC*** will ensure completion of both vertical and horizontal line of communications within the structural organization of the social communications ministry of the Church.

The possible activities of a PCC:

1. Allocate a specific place in the church premises:

    - To accommodate a showroom-cum-sales-counter

type of space/place to store and display audiovisual consumer/ retail materials like pictures, audio, video cassettes and CDs.

- To display and make available current magazines and catholic publications and other relevant materials connected specifically with communication media.

2. Appoint volunteers for the proper preparation and display of the Parish Bulletin, and oversee to its regular updating.

3. Facilitate regular screening of religious and audiovisual programs, specifically during Lenten and Christmas seasons and on other festivals and occasion of Parish level celebrations.

4. Liaise between the parish and the diocesan centre for organizing Multi-media shows on different themes at different occasions to enhance and strengthen the quality of spiritual and community life of the parish.

5. Help organize the annual 'Communication Day' at the parish level, every year.

6. Promote radio-listeners' clubs in the parish for both the Vatican Radio as well as for the Radio Veritas Asia.

7. Select talented youth, and recommend them to the diocesan communications authority for their training and promotions in the field of communication media.

8. Cooperate with other apostolic wing of the Parish by supporting them on the matters of social communication.

The ***PCC*** may be subjected to a short course of training in communication, so that it is better equipped to carry out the functions of the ***PCC***.

(Inspiration received for this write-up: Pastoral Course in Communication, Gregorian University, Rome)

[Fr.Arun Ignatius Abraham, sj, is Director of the BIJHAN Regional Communications Centre – Ravi Bharti, Patna and Secretary of the Commission for Social Communications of the Bihar – Jharkhand Catholic Bishops' Council.]

•••

Church's Right to Use Media

"It is the Church's birthright to use and own any of these media which are necessary or useful for the formation of Christians and for pastoral activity. Pastors of soul have the task of instructing and directing the faithful how to use these media in a way that will ensure their own salvation and perfection and that of all mankind."

(Inter Mirifica, n. 3)

7

NETWORKING AND NEWS-SHARING

7.1

NETWORKING AND NEWS SHARING AMONG PUBLICATIONS

Fr George Veliparambil

Each Newspaper is bound to have its own scope of coverage and has to address a particular audience. This is necessary in order to ensure the nature, character and permanence of a newspaper and to sustain readership and interest.

Historically Catholic newspapers were meant to be apologetic, defensive and propagandist. We have to stop for a moment and examine whether or not we have shed these characteristics. We may divide newspapers into the following categories:

A.

1. Church periodicals (traditional publications which have more or less the same contents, format and routine matter like articles on faith and morals, notices and

information, news of church personnel, activities and the like)
2. Diocesan (congregation or mission) Bulletins or organs (notices and information, events and engagement)
3. The new generation publication with a window to the world (trying to engage with topics affecting the everyday life of the people and the nation from the point of view of the Church and the Church's teaching)

The first two types are well known to us.

The third one is the group of new publications attempting to open a window to the world.

B.

Have Church publications changed their nature of being defensive, apologetic and sectarian in the last fifty years? If not, why?

C.

1. What role does public opinion play in the running of our publications? "Public opinion within the Church" was the theme of the UCIP World Congress in Rupholding, Germany in 1989. Has the Church in India or the managements of the newspapers in India ever thought of public opinion within the Church? Has it any apparatus to do this? Has it tried to gauge it? Do the church publications give a try even among the staff members?

2. Two important documents of the Church - "*Communio et Progressio*" (1971) and *Aetatis Novae* (1992) refer to the importance of Public Relations in the Church, both internal and external, not as a tool for business promotion

but as a "witness of Christians and Christian communities to the value of the kingdom of God" (FABC Bandung Meeting). It should be transparent, dialogic and marked by candour.

D.

Do the church publications plunge into the several issues facing the Church and the nation? Such as

The Church:

1. Church administration
2. Administration of temporalities
3. Administration of institutions
4. Use of funds
5. Rite and Jurisdiction
6. Celibacy of the priests and the religious
7. Training of the clergy

The Nation:

1. General elections
2. Economics
3. Globalization
4. Market Liberalization
5. Ecology
6. Consumerism
7. Alternatives to the mainstream systems

Public opinion must still be one of our primary concerns.

The church press can think of networking and sharing of news only if and when we have fixed our area of coverage and scope.

If we wish to have any say in forming public opinion in the nation, the first thing to do is to enter the national stream of newspapers. We have not yet entered that arena. Our biggest attempt has reached the stature of the "Indian Currents" and has stayed there. Can any amount of good will and good wish make any newspaper enter the national stream? Until we have a national stream newspaper we can hardly think of networking and sharing of news on a national level. We do not mean that the church as a whole or even the hierarchy should come forward and set up a national newspaper. Some attempt has been made on these lines. Can the hierarchy support such initiatives in a big and meaningful manner? There are half a dozen Catholic newspapers in the country which have their specific area and scope at least in a hazy manner. Could these initiatives be stabilized, consolidated, strengthened and made vibrant? We have one national newsgathering apparatus. What have we staked to make it professional, viable and serviceable? In any country news agencies are initiated, supported and maintained by the newspapers themselves. What about the news agency in India? The newspapers should come forward and take over the news agency, make it accountable to them, run it according to their requirements. Then, why shy away?

E.

If we look at the secular newspaper world, we can note two striking traits:

1. Increasing competition to increase circulation and revenue
2. Professional collaboration to improve quality and to cut cost

I think we have to start somewhere and the time is today.

[Having served as the Editor of the Kerala Times, Fr. George Veliparambil, has been in the field of print media for long time. Presently he is the Managing Director of the South Asian Religious News (SAR News) and the President of the South Asian Catholic Press Association.]

...

7.2

SHARING NEWS

Fr Francis D'Britto

1. Four modern Gospels

Because of the advanced technology, news travels at the speed of light into the global village. Television and internet has brought the world in our drawing room. Like the angel Gabriel, the news channels are bringing to us the news, though not always the good news.

We must be grateful to God for the modern means of communication. In theology we speak of 'continuous creative act of God' and his constant self revelation. God is speaking to us through the four major sources of communication e.g. Printed word, Radio, film, Television & internet etc. These four have become the modern Gospels! Barring films the three sources are constantly pouring in news.

2. Church - The generator of Good News

In India, the church is one of the biggest NGO's. It has got a huge Network of healthcare, education & social work. Many noval and extra ordinary programmes are conducted by thc church related organizations. Take for example the marriage preparation courses, engaged and marriage encounters etc. The society at large will certainly benefit from it.

The church related agencies are constantly interacting with all sorts of people. They have been daily generating a lot of news but unfortunately it is not highlighted as it should have been.

3. Are we Media-shy?

Perhaps because of the false idea of humility we prefer to remain 'in cognitu'. Some of our religious leaders seem to be media shy. Some Bishops and superiors are not comfortable with media persons. A person who possesses truth is fearless and is ready to share the good news he has. All democratic societies today respect the right to information. The decree on the instruments of social communication states, "Hence there exists within human society a right to information about affairs which affect men individually or collectively and according to the circumstances of each. The proper exercise of this right demands that the matter communicated always be true and as complete as charity and justice allow. The manner of communication should furthermore be honorable and appropriate this means that in the gathering and publication of news the norms of morality and the legitimate rights and dignity of a man must be held sacred. For knowledge is sometimes unprofitable, but charity edifies." (No 5)

Our Lord tells us that "Men do not light a lamp and put it under a bushel but on a lamp stand and it gives light to all in the house." The church is the city that is situated on the hill and it cannot remain hidden. In case we are tempted to close the city gates, only the bad news will spread.

4. Sharing News

The Lord has given us the mandate to communicate the Good News to the entire creation. Nearly every diocese has a news bulletin, which contains the news of the dioceses. The dioceses of the region should share the news with each other.

Suvarta the diocesan monthly of Vasai covers news as follows:-

- International News:
  Sources: Zenit, Vatican Radio & The Tablet

- The Church in India:
  Source: SAR News, UCAN

- Western Region News:
  Source: The diocesan bulletins

- Local News:
  Source: Reporters and Parish Bulletins

5. News Sharing with the secular media

The church, as said earlier, generates a lot of news but we do not know how to share it. There is something like news marketing. In order to disseminate news, we need to take the following steps immediately.

- Appoint a PRO for every diocese. He should be a person who is well versed in vernacular language. Above all he should be a media friendly person. He has to constantly keep in touch with the news agencies & news editors.

- Be quick: In the field of media, everything is wanted yesterday! Hence we must release news as soon as possible, especially for the daily newspapers. E.g. The Christmas message of the local Bishops should reach to the Press office by the afternoon on 24th December. Kindly attach a photo of the Bishop. It is advisable to personally hand over the news to the news editor who usually is on his desk after 2.00 p.m.

- Invite local reporters for important functions in your institutions. Be friendly with them. At least once a year call them for modest tea party.

- Try to avoid being apologetic and propagandist.

- Issue an immediate press release when great event take place e.g. death of a great religious or national leader, the festivals of various religions etc.

In short, the church in India has a lot of news to share. Let's share it these "The world may see your good works and give glory to your Father who is in heaven."(Matt 5, 16)

[Fr.Francis D'Britto is the editor of popular Marathi periodical – Suvarta. Both as a social activist and journalist, he has won many awards.]

Call to be Vigilant

"Necessary discretion is to be observed in the use of media of social communication, and whatever is harmful to one's vocation and dangerous to the chastity of a consecrated person is to be avoided."

(Canon 666)

8

DISTRIBUTION SYSTEM FOR MEDIA PRODUCTIONS AND PUBLICATIONS

8.1

A STRATEGY FOR DISTRIBUTION

Sr Anne Plathara, dsp

In today's world the service industry is growing much faster than the manufacturing industry. Organizations are rapidly becoming aware that consumers are growing more and demanding more. So they are going out of their way to create intangible services which surround the core product or brand. So a Hindustan Lever agent will not rest satisfied with just advertising a soap or a shampoo but will try and deliver it directly to your house. The underlying logic is that if a customer feels that he does not have to unnecessarily inconvenience himself in obtaining Hindustan Lever brands then he will patronize Hindustan Lever brands more than brands from other companies. This additional service of reaching the product to one's doorstep is part of the distribution service strategy which Companies are now employing. It is because distribution is now seen as a critically important factor. The products or brands which a Company produces need to be easily accessible to potential customers. Access is today's buzzword and Distribution creates the Access touch points for the Company and customer.

In this context what we find in the Church is that there is hardly any attention paid to 'distribution' in comparison to 'production'. We seem to have invested and become somewhat proficient in production. But one finds an inadequate focus given to distribution. Distribution is the unglamorous part of marketing and yet such a critical part. This is seen in the *Dabbawallas* of Mumbai daily delivering food to thousands of people in Mumbai with no error. The Prince of Wales was awestruck and now the ordinary *dabbawalla* is giving lectures to the doyens of business on Distribution strategy. Distribution fulfills the effort of production by ensuring that all 'productions' reach the relevant audiences. Today in a world ridden with complexity we need to discern which channels one can use to distribute our 'productions'. I will attempt to suggest a few.

Firstly, we already have existing Pauline book centres. In these outlets we keep not only books but also CD-ROMS and music cassettes. One can utilize these outlets to store the various productions which are created. The irony in today's world is that even though sales of books and cassettes and various other media formats is taking place through Internet sites like Amazon.com still people are flocking to bookstores because the bookstore offers a certain ambience of quiet and leisure for browsing which is a delectable experience and which cannot be replaced by the experience of purchasing on the Net. Our bookstores are well-known for disseminating religious books and other media 'productions'. Our bookstores also offer this calm and peaceful atmosphere which people seek when they are evaluating a book or cassette or CD-ROM to purchase.

What we also find today is that customers as a result of being pandered to want a greater and greater choice of the same content and formats being made available through different channels of distribution. So even if books or Cassettes or CD-ROMs are available through our bookstores, still the customer expects the same to be available through other channels of distribution too. Therefore, we need to look for other channels of distribution. The customer today is driven by his need to access everything a Company offers in the most convenient manner.

Our Sisters go to various parishes and schools. This becomes a very personalized way of reaching out to relevant audiences especially teachers and students. We already carry with us on our visits to schools and parishes Media Productions of other Congregations too. This effort can be consolidated. In fact, these visits can be transformed into events which could be organized as Book Exhibition fairs in schools and where even parents avail of this opportunity of purchasing books or cassettes or CD-ROMs or DVDs, as the case may be.

Today the customer is no longer looking at the plain purchase of just a book or a cassette or a CD-ROM. He is looking for an overall experience which he has in the context of his purchases, be it books or CD-ROMs or DVDs and so on. A pleasant experience is the differentiator which will make him either choose to purchase a particular product or brand or not purchase it. So book exhibition fairs are becoming an ideal vehicle for delivering this pleasant experience. However, a book exhibition event could be treated as a *Mela,* where not only books or CDs or DVDs or cassettes are placed for sale but there are also reviews and panel discussions and educational videos which are shown and talks given on various topics as well as live readings by authors going on. It's like food festival where a delicious spread of various dishes is offered from which one is induced to choose.

All Congregations need to be involved in organizing and participating in such a *Melas*. Such a *Mela,* if held every year, it becomes a much anticipated distribution platform for all our productions. Such *Melas* can be organized at different levels. At the parish or deanery level or at the school level or at the common diocesan level.

Lastly, we need to make a concerted effort to exploit the channel of the Internet. Many of our Congregations have their own websites. One way of doing this is to individually set up within one's own website a listing of all the productions which the Congregation intends to put up for sale and arrange for a payment mechanism. Usually people don't trust paying through the Net by revealing their credit card number. So acceptance of cheques could be a feasible possibility. But if one promotes the Net as a Channel of distribution, then one needs to make people aware of the same by advertising in relevant publications to draw them to the website. Also one needs to have a warehouse where one can store all the productions and distribute them through courier or post as the case may be.

In conclusion, I would like to stress the criticality of distribution in achieving the dissemination of all the excellent productions which wc have. We have long been talking about networking and collaborating. This is an ideal opportunity for us to come together and examine these proposals so that they can be adopted by all of us.

[Sr Anne Plathara, dsp is the Provincial Superior of the Daughters of St. Paul, Mumbai.]

8.2

DISTRIBUTION SYSTEM FOR MEDIA PRODUCTIONS

Fr Darryl D'Souza, sdb

A director of a company said, "I don't understand? I cringe when I think that we are paying more to our marketing vice president than our company's President." The chairman replied, "How is it that you don't understand? Without the sales that come through marketing - we wouldn't need a president - or anyone else for that matter!" Yes marketing does in fact have a significant effect on our media houses being financially viable.

Though marketing is a larger process, I will dwell on the topic that has been given to me namely: "Evolving a distribution system for media products", which is an important and essential step in marketing.

An essential method to scout market opportunities for your product or service is to study social and business trends. New social trends transform how goods are built and sold. Business opportunities grow out of the changes in the social order.

Back in the 1920s, who would have thought that bottled water will be big business? With the growing consciousness for cleaner and healthier living, smart marketers correctly predicted that people would want to drink bottled water as against water straight from the tap. And who would have guessed that the Internet would be a big thing that it is today, changing everything that we know about doing business?

The challenge for the catholic media production house will be to see if it can find business opportunities in the trends that society passes through, some upcoming ones of which are presented below:

Increasing globalization of business – The companies that will excel in the 21st century will be the ones that build down the global barriers. Spurred by the growing acceptance of the internet, globalization is one of the biggest trends today and will continue to accelerate in the coming years. Do catholic media production houses build barriers or competition or selfishness (my productions)? Is the internet being sufficient utilized to 'market God', His outlook?

Mass customization - Huge conglomerates are beginning to offer products that could be customized by potential buyers based on his or her preferences. Hence, the customers get what they want at prices acceptable to them. Consider what that means for opportunities in businesses providing products or services individually tailored to each customer. Can we think of ways of entering into customization of religious media products so that Christian families can get things of their choice?

Reinvention of religion - As people continue to cast off traditional beliefs and services, others return to them even more vigorously. Consider what that means for opportunities in books, tapes, CD's, DVD's, MP3's, broadcasting, cable opportunities and online services.

Yearning for high-tech products and services - This includes the nostalgia induced by high-tech solutions to everything. Consider what that means to folk media, symbols, and non-mainstream media.

Increasing power of women - The increased purchasing power of women is also evident on the Internet, marketing or in print or electronic journalism or secular products made with women as target.

Network development - The social mechanism has undergone a change. Economic activities beyond geographical constraints are a reality, thereby levelling differences among various regions. Information transmission on networks is allowing joint social activities, and stratified communities beyond regions, cultures, fields or generations are being formed. Opening of information will further increase the transparency and fairness of the social system. Does this pose a challenge to our own church networks especially the network between catholic and Christian media houses?

Understanding such trends, can we take some reflections for our consideration in terms of distribution?

It is important to first answer the question to ourselves: Am I a pastor (including women religious) or a business person in my outlook or mentality? As Jesus said: "Where your treasure lies, there will your heart be also." And our decisions will be easily coloured by one or the other.

A Catholic/Christian media producer is first a Pastor and then a business person, more so for a priests and religious.

Can catholic media houses develop a sense of belonging to each other rather compete. We have to compete, but with the secular market (apparently we cannot because of their strength in reach, economics and attitude; but think of it,.the co-ordinated network of the catholic media is larger) and in unity, projcct thc valucs of thc Lord Jesus to Catholics and others.

Do our Media products arise out of the needs of the people? Do they answer their needs/desires? This can be gauged from research on the world social, religious, educational, moral, catechetical or political trends.

• There is a false notion or perception even by church personnel that the marketing of media products (i.e. selling media products) is purely business). However it is primarily a ministry of distribution of Christian life and evangelizing and catechizing or teaching through media forms.

Globalisation has led to the opening up of national and regional boundaries. Can we think of the geographical hub of Christian worship for the family i.e. the local church, the parish as the outlet where the Christian family will have access to media productions and publications? Can we therefore think if "every parish" having a media outlet. Here the Bishops, in their pastoral letters, have an influential role in encouraging parish priests to open mini media outlets or invite media houses to exhibit their products for the faithful.

Why only parishes, we can also think of Christian schools which are so accessible even to people of other faiths. Think of the good that can be done by making Christian media products within the access of people of other faiths.

As seen today, production centres or book centres are not within the easy reach and access of our target i.e. families. Our productions are for the family. The family is the primary focus of our evangelization or catechetical activity. Can we think of flooding the Christian family with Christian media products by allowing them easy access to our reduction in terms of reach?

Specialised material for priests, religious, teachers, schools, social centres etc. can be accessed from catholic media bookshops. But family based catholic material should be available in parish media outlets.

We are in the era of coalitions. Can we have interactions among catholic publishers and producers to meet, share to "forge alliances" (in religious sense of networking) for e.g. about translations.

Can we have a policy on copyright, a common understanding on this matter?

Can we think of a central agency which can distribute or channelise productions of the media houses to different regions or media outlets? This will ensure greater reach of catholic productions where they are needed. Individual houses may or may not have the reach or personnel. Hence the products are either not sold or much money is spent on unnecessary adverts rather than necessary ones and accessibility is minimal. But worse, the productions are not known at all.

Can we look at Signis India to facilitate such distribution by setting up a wing fulfilling this business need with of course a fee or commission?

[Fr. Darryl D'Souza, sdb is the Secretary of BOSCOM South Asia and director of Tej- Prasarini Don Bosco Communications at Mumbai. Also he is the Provincial co-ordinator of Bosco Information Service. He has been editing a magazine called SDB West.]

...

8.3

A DISTRIBUTION MECHANISM

Fr Dominic Emmanuel, svd

What is marketing?

- Marketing is a social and managerial process whereby individuals and groups obtain what they need and want through creating and exchanging products and value (money) with others.

- We need to clarify that the fields of productions and marketing are two entirely different fields, independent of each other. We have the example of books sold by Daughters of St. Paul or Fathers/Brothers of St. Paul. They have clearly defined roles of who is involved in productions and who in sales (distribution). There are sisters who are constantly on the move selling books or products.

- To do that they produce enough number of books or cassettes regularly.

- Can our media centres afford to do this? In other words would we be able to produce enough for regular sales and distribution? But this is also product specific. For instance, Indian Currents is a product that is being produced weekly and very regularly. They can afford to do that. But the example of Indian Currents cannot be applied to our other media productions like our CDs, videos, audio cassettes and so on.

- So we need to understand and if possible evolve a new strategy?

The need for constant Research and updating

- An important area in terms of marketing for productions is Research at various levels.

- For instance, reaching a pre-production or pre-publication understanding (agreement) with people in the marketing field or media distribution outlets.

- We need to also keep updating from time to time according to the changing times, needs, tastes and preferences of our target group.

- We must find out as to how convenient it is for people to use what we produce. This is all part of research.

- It is also important for us to assess who our competitors in the field are.

- The presentation of a product for instance, the colour scheme; the quality of paper for books or film quality is another factor that needs to be looked into if we would like our product to sell.

What makes marketing easy?

- Marketing can never be isolated from the risk involved in any kind of production. In other words one can never be sure of success. Like the film I am making. Films made by famous film producers like Mahesh Bhatt also flop, even though they have long experience and are adept at making them.

- Marketing also becomes easy when the product is of quality to the customer.

- So I go back to two points that I made in my last presentation and would like to reiterate that one would find it easier to sell ones product if it is produced with professional quality. So we fall back on the all important quality of professionalism. It becomes again the keyword.

- The other keyword used in our previous presentation is Networking.

[Rev. Dr. Dominic Emmanuel, svd, is presently the Spokesperson and Director of the Communication/Information Bureau of the Delhi Catholic Archdiocese. He is the President of Signis India and has been involved in broadcasting over Radio Veritas Asia and Jain TV Channel. He has to his credit nearly 200 articles in the national dailies in Hindi and English.]

...

Call for Fresh Energy and Imagination

"The history of evangelization is not just a matter of geographic expansion, for the Church has also had to cross many cultural thresholds, each of which called for fresh energy and imagination in proclaiming the one Gospel of Jesus Christ. The age of the great discoveries, the Renaissance and the invention of printing, the Industrial Revolution and the birth of the modern world: these, too, were threshold moments that demanded new forms of evangelization. Now, with the communications and information revolution in full swing, the Church stands unmistakably at another decisive gateway."

(John Paul II, World Communications Day 2002)

9

PROMOTING ALTERNATIVE MEDIA

9.1

MISSION AND ALTERNATIVE MEDIA

Fr Eugene

Introduction

The Church in India is called to be a communicating Church. Today we notice an exploding growth and availability of communications media for enriching the lives not only of individuals but also of society at large. It is also true that the people with whom we are working are in the grip of media. While providing "unlimited opportunities for information, education, cultural expansion and even spiritual growth, media also have the capacity to do grave harm by presenting an inadequate or even deformed outlook on life, on religion, on morality" etc *(Pope John Paul II)*. Therefore it is immensely important that a right understanding of and positive use of media is amply enhanced in the Church.

Communication of Jesus

Let us examine the way Jesus communicated with his audience. He spoke in pictures: light, salt, lamp, net, coin, mustard seed, fig tree, living water, vine, straying sheep, the sower and the seed and so on. "He taught nothing without the use of parables." (Mt. 13, 34). "In order to have a credible and ideal communication, he accepted his listeners as they were. Communication as a process can occur between two equal beings. He went to the place where they were. He engaged in the listeners' communication process. At times his communication began by listening to his opponents or his hearers and thereby engaging along with them in their search for meaning in life and of God rather than simply asking them to comply with his own meanings of God and of life. Thereby Jesus engaged in public communication in the way people expected, presenting his meanings among a wide range of meanings that were available to his hearers. Jesus used different types of communication that were familiar to his hearers which also reflected their contemporary context." *(Joshva Raja, Mission Today VI (2004), 222)*

Media with a 'human face'

The above reflections naturally take the focus on to the need and importance of the alternative media in the mission of the Church: **Indian dance and music, folk art, street theatre** etc. No doubt the high speed information technology has come to stay and it can not be undermined nor sidelined by the alternative media. Our concern should be to develop a media with a '**human face**' along side the mainstream techno-media. The kingdom of God comes to a people who are profoundly linked to a culture, and the building of the kingdom cannot avoid applying elements from human cultures.

Incarnation itself is communication between God and man. It is aptly right, therefore, the media that we engage in communicating the good news of Incarnation have a strong and visible **component of human elements**. In answering the call to be a communicating Church, she should "become an intelligible sign of what she is" (RM.52) and be **at home** in this land of rich cultural heritage and of major world religions.

Suggestions for developing alternative media:

- To start with, church schools must promote Indian dance and music as part of the curriculum. An environment of Indian culture in the schools makes a good impact on the society around. The medium itself can be the message.
- It is also possible to develop interest for street theatre among school children and use it as a medium for education at various occasions in schools.
- Awareness should be created in formation houses towards the value and usefulness of performing art and street theatre. Seminarians and persons in formation should be sensitized and equipped to use them in their future ministry.
- At parish level, boys and girls with aptitude and talent can be formed into a group, given basic training and organized into a performing troupe. Such a troupe can be given ongoing formation during vacation in order to present biblical and social awareness programs.
- Diocesan catechetical centres should take initiative to coordinate the talents from schools and parishes so as to promote the use of alternative media at every sphere of church's life. Diocesan Bible Day, Youth Day, Peace Day, Communications Day etc. can be occasions for promoting effective use of such media.
- Diocesan social work centres must have a trained – permanent team for street theatre and folk art like puppetry. This is a tested and proved medium for community building

and awareness education at grass root level.

- Regional Pastoral/ Communication Centre must make every effort to build up professional resources for this task and offer its services to schools, parishes and diocesan centres for training as well as performances.
- Regional Commission for Communication should play an inspirational role in strengthening the centres in the region. Indian Communications Day can be used as an opportunity to organize regional level programmes for promoting this cause.

[Fr. Eugene is the Director of the Regional Pastoral Centre - Nav Sadhana. He is also the Director of the Nav Sadhana College of Fine Arts, Varanasi.]

...

9.2

FOSTERING ALTERNATIVE MEDIA FOR PROCLAMATION

Fr Denis D'Sa

A story is told of a naturalist and a banker strolling together along a noisy street. Suddenly the naturalist grabbed the hand of his companion and said, "Do you here a cricket chirping?" The banker ridiculed the idea that anyone could hear such noises in that traffic din. But the naturalist proved that he was right when a spotted a cricket among the vegetables in a push cart. A step further the banker halted his companion and said, "Someone has dropped a coin." The naturalist scoffed at the idea but the banker pointed to a coin on the footpath a few steps further! So, communication is effective in each ones cultural context. There can be no communication possible in cultural vacuum. Cultural norms and attitudes of people are sensitive aspects and they have vital role to play in any act of communication. None of these cultural issues can be ignored when communication strategies are planned.

To make any communication effective in rural and tribal areas, traditional folk media or the alternative media have a very important role to play. Although there is a technological revolution in the electronic media, for much of the masses they are out of reach. In this context, the alternate media like the drama, dance, folk arts, theatre etc. bring about a sense of cultural unity, they are more appealing to the masses because they are a part of their everyday life. Time and again it is noticed that people understand messages clearly when expressed in a medium familiar to them. Themes like health, hygiene, environment, family planning, development etc. when conveyed to through a folk song, drama, dance, puppet show, street play etc. reach them better.

Why?

- They are intimate to the masses
- They are in the language of the masses
- Their appeal is primarily to the emotions and not the intellect
- There is a variety in them
- They are local, they are alive and dynamic
- They are easily available and flexible to accommodate new themes
- They are acceptable to a variety of audiences
- They are low cost
- They are the people's media

Yet there is a danger that these alternative media be neglected by the church because of the onslaught of the electronic media (which are colourful, city based and impressive) and electronic gadgets. The church has to pay attention to the development of the folk media, training people in the alternative media, identifying those already in this media, preservation and documentation of these media, because much of India is still rural.

Action plan

1. Academic level - university courses:

   There are many centres like Kalai Kaviri, Nav Sadhana, Sandesha etc that are offering graduation and post graduation courses in the arts like dance, drama, singing, and other performing arts. These are really the cultural centres that have tremendous influence among the people of other faiths. The Registrar of Mangalore University was saying ones, "Sandesha College of Fine Arts may be a small one, but it commands great respect and influence, more than many of the established colleges." Such centres need to be strengthened. Many of our church personnel who show an aptitude in these arts, could be trained in these places and then sent for specialization. In fact, these are the public relations and dialogue centres for the Church. Inter-culturally, many other dioceses can take a clue from these centres and have a similar centre of their own.

2. Diploma or certificate or crash courses could be offered as it is done in Sangeeth Abhinay Academy, Karnataka Kala Kendra, National Biblical, Catechetical and Liturgical Centre, Kalai Kaviri, Nav Sadhana and Prem Sanchar Kendra.

3. Research and documentation of folk songs for future generation: Dr. B.S. Talwadi of Karnataka has done his research in this area and has published several books. We need to encourage such initiatives, lest our folk tradition dies out.

4. Many biblical or value based themes could be presented through the folk media. Yakshagana on the Life of Jesus,

Life of St Antony etc. are some of the successful ventures. They are excellent tools for evangelization in the people' media.

5. A taste for the folk, traditional arts and the other alternative media should bc givcn to children at an early age. How? Through -

   - Cultural festivals (*Kalotsava*), festival of dance, patriotic and classical songs, folk songs and folk dances, drama etc.
   - Cultural competitions.
   - Introducing these subjects in the school curriculum in schools under our management.
   - Performing these art forms during school days and other national festivals.
   - Having an audio-visual library of these folk arts.
   - Cultural exchange programs/ workshops.
   - Street theatre workshops.

6. Seminary Level

   - Subjects like theatre, dance, music and other alternate media should be introduced in the seminary program, so that when they go out to communicate the message of Christ, they would be able to contextualize and communicate in a medium of the people.
   - To use them in faith formation and proclamation.
   - Dance and music and drama could be introduced in worship.
   - Drama associations could be formed in parishes which can perform at weekends.
   - Seminarians could be sent for graduation and post graduation studies in these art forms.
   - Encourage specialisation in dance and music and other performing arts.

- Promote composition and choreography of ballets on Jesus' life such as *Jyotirgamaya, Yesu Krist Jayanthi 2000, Navodaya*, Harmony and so on.
- Bhajans like the ones composed by Frs. Charles vas and Felix Noronha could be promoted.
- Encourage programmes like Bible Magic by Fr. Ivan Madtha which offers Edu-tainment.
- Identify and recognise folk artistes through awards.
- Organize Folk Art Festivals by inviting folk artistes to perform and exchange views
- Provide scholarships to study folk arts for rural talents.
- Collaboration with Janapada Academy, ICCR, and other organizations.

Folk arts or the alternative media are closely intermingled with everyday life, in festivals, religious ceremonies, rituals etc. If we want to be effective among the masses, we need to preserve, promote and propagate these alternate media.

[Fr. Denis D'Sa is Director of the Karnataka Regional Communications Centre – SANDESHA and Director of the Sandesha College of Fine Arts, Mangalore.]

...

9.3

STREET THEATRE AND THE *AWAAZ* TROUPE

Fr John Paul Herman, svd

Comparison

MASS MEDIA MEDIA	ALTERNATIVE/GROUP/ FOLK
• Media explosion/ new phenomenon	* Part of life/ traditional
• Mass audiences	* Community/ group audiences
• One way communication	* Two-way/ interactive
• Technology based	* Traditional art forms - story, folk dance, song, folk drama etc.
• Expensive/ skilled	* Low cost/ learnt by practice
• Elitist/ controlled by the powerful	* Belong to the marginalized/ poor

• Dehumanising/ materialistic	* Enabling values
• Commercial interest	* Building a community
• Reach through sounds and images	* Direct through verbal/ non verbal
• Audience are mere observers/ passive	* Audience participate actively
• Individualistic	* Community based
• Create public opinion	* Mould public opinion

Positive influence of Mass Media

- Globalization
- Also used for developmental purposes-education, human issued etc.

Therefore Mass media is important and powerful but it leaves out a big section of the people.

Need:

So- we need to equally highlight mass media and alternative media because both are powerful and important. Therefore, while we focus on mainstream media, we also need to stress this neglected alternate which are in abundant use among the poorer sections of the society. Besides they are-

- Full of variety, beautiful and creative
- Contribute in building community
- Facilitate the change in society
- Facilitate the change in society
- Are popular and people's media
- This is a medium of the poor, weak, marginalized and voice of the voiceless.

Relevance

Street Play was started in China against communism rule where people had no voice in decision making. From China it came to India. Though it is not very old form of media, it incorporates various forms of fold media as folk dance, music and song, etc.

Even today in this age of sophisticated technologies- folk media is important and powerful. It does appeal both in cities and remote areas. Street theatre is very effective even in a metropolis such as New Delhi.

AWAAZ Troupe

When I was appointed director of archdiocesan Media Commission, I came across some youth who were interested to do something. This germinated the idea to form a street play group. We organized a training programme, in which 15 participated. After the training the group got busy with preparing their own plays. And the first play was performed by this group called *AWAAZ* on India Communications Day in the year 2000. And from that day till today, the group has performed more than 50 plays on various issues like- unity in the church (*Paanch Unguliyan*), on rites (*Ek Aur Soolie*), communal harmony (*Gadda*), positive use of communication(Athwa Sanskar),election awareness (*Satta Ka Khel*) and corruption (*Khazana*).

Ek Aur Soolie, Gadda, and *Satta Ka Khel* became great hits. Seeing the profound impact, the group is now even more determined and has taken another step to translate the motivation into action. The next project is ready to he launched on 15th of August2004. It is on corruption and would be implemented in collaboration with a NGO called 'Parivarthan', who actually take up such cases and work for it.

Strategy of the group

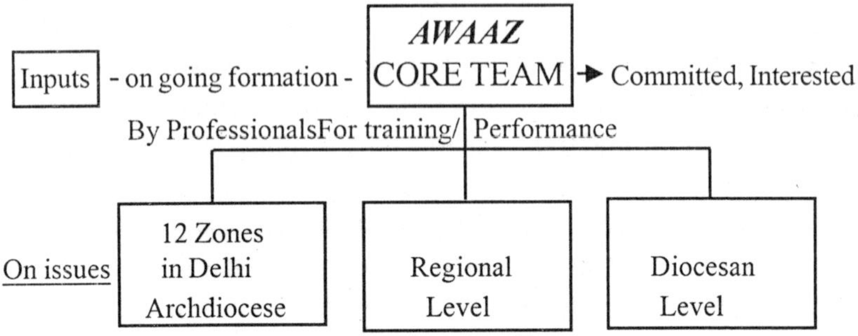

- Commitment
- Christian approach
- Advance training
- Updating etc.

Diocesan level - Local issues
- Reaching out to grassroots(parishes)

Regional level - In different dioceses of the region

National level - In association with CBCI and other regions

AIM
- Change in society-awareness against social evils, one's responsibilities
- Building Kingdom of God based on equality, Justice and Peace, which is the Mission of Church

INCENTIVE - Change in themselves - Awareness of issues (Election, corruption, Unity, Communal harmony, Rite issues)
- Working for a cause
- Commitment
- Responsibility

Involvement

Media persons	- Resource persons /Publicity
Youth	- performance
Associations	- Arrangements
Parish priests/ other priests	- Homily
Committed/activists	- Inputs/feedback
NGO and other Christian organisations	- Networking

Expenses

- Training
- Transport
- Food
- Dress and pops
- Refreshment for practice & TA

Criteria

- Commitment & interest

Publicity

- Secular news papers, TV channels, Christian Organisations, UCAN, CBCI, RCC, DCP and Christian Publications.

Future plan

At the national level in association with CBCI, at the regional level with RCC, at the diocesan level with the help of parish priest and at the zonal level with the help of zonal co-ordinators and youth animators.

[Fr. John Paul is presently the Director of the Archdiocesan Media Commission and Secretary of the Northern Regional Commission.]

...

11. ADDRESSES

11.1 CBCI Commission for Social Communications

Chairman

Abp Oswald Gracias
(P) Archbishop of Agra
Cathedral House
Wazirpura Road
Agra - 282 003.

T : (0562) 21 51 318, 25 26 397
F : (0562) 21 53 939
M: 098370 56223
E : abpossie@sancharnet.in

Members

Bp Antony Devotta
Bishop of Tiruchirapalli
Bishop's House
P. B. 14, 12A Convent Road
Tiruchirapalli - 620 001.

T : (0431) 41 56 35, 40 10 14 (P)
F : (0431) 41 75 02
E: trichidio@eth.net

Bp Leo Cornelio, svd
Bishop of Khandwa
Bishop's House
Khandwa - 450 001
MADHYA PRADESH.

T : (0733) 22 22 935, 22 23 603 (P)
F : (0733) 22 24 038
M: 098260 67823
E : lcornel@sancharnet.in

Executive Secretary

Fr Henry D'Souza
CBCI Centre
1, Ashok Place
New Delhi - 110 001.

T: (011) 23 34 84 23, 23 34 44 70
M: 093137 82685
E: cbcimo@bol.net.in
W: www.cbcisite.com

11.2 Regional Commissions

Agra Region

Chairman
Bp Patrick Paul D'Souza
Bishop's House
45, Varanasi Cantt.
Varanasi – 221 002.

T: (0542) 25 04 235, 25 00 043 (P)
F: (0542) 25 02 767
M: 094152 25582
E: dovns@sify.com

Secretary
Fr Antony Muthu
Nav Sadhana, Tarna
Shivpur Post, Varanasi – 221 003.

T: (0542) 22 84 160, 22 83 072
E: sadhana_vns@sify.com

Andhra Region

Chairman
Bp Johannes Gorantla
Bishop's House
B. Camp, Kurnool - 518 002.

T: (08518) 27 03 93, 27 68 12 (P)
F: (08518) 27 03 13
E: pgorantla1@rediffmail.com

Secretary
Fr David Raju
Amruthavani
P. B. 1588, 50 Sebastian Rd
Secunderabad – 500 003.

T: (040) 77 03 968, 77 01 156
F: (040) 77 00 957
E: amruthavani@hotmail.com

Bengal Region

Chairman
Bp Joseph Suren Gomes
Bishop's House
P.O. Krishnagar
Krishnagar - 741 101.

T: (03472) 25 25 54 (O), 25 26 64 (P)
F: (03472) 25 26 64
E: bpjgomes@vsnl.net

Secretary
Fr P.J. Joseph, sj
Chitrabani, 76 Rafi Ahmed
Kidwai Rd, Kolkata – 700 016.

T: (033) 22 44 01 08 (O)
F: (033) 22 45 15 07
E: cbcal@cal.vsnl.net.in

Bijhan Region

Chairman
Bp Vincent Barwa
Auxiliary Bishop of Ranchi
Archbishop's House, Purulia Road
P.B. 5, Ranchi - 834 001.

T: (0651) 2204 728, 2201 684 (P)
F: (0651) 23 04 844
M: 098101 31552
E: vincent-barwa@rediffmail.com

Secretary
Fr Arun Ignatius Abraham
Ravi Bharti Institute
Post Sadaquat Asharam
Patna – 800 010.

T: (0612) 26 34 55, 26 22 84
E: ravibharti@sancharnet.in

Karnataka Region

Chairman
Bp Aloysius Paul D' Souza
Bishop's House
Kodialbail Post
Mangalore– 575 003.

T: (0824) 24 40 524, 24 40 421(P)
F: (0824) 24 44 035
E: bishopap@sancharnet.in

Secretary
Fr Denis D'Sa
Sandesha, Premnagar
Bajjodi, Mangalore - 575 005.

T: (0824) 22 13 278
M: 094480 26540
E: sandesha_d@yahoo.co.in

Kerala Region

Chairman
Bp Thomas Chakiath
Aux. Bp of Ernakulam-A'mly
Major Archbishop's House
P. B. No. 2580, Cochin - 682 031.

T: (0484) 23 52 629, 23 52 906
F : (0484) 23 55 010
E: bpchakiath@hotmail.com

Secretary
Fr Devassy Kollamkudyil
KCBC Media Comm., POC
P. B. 2251, Palarivattom
Kochi – 682 025.

T: (0484) 28 06 227, 28 05 815
M: (0484) 32 92 622
E: mediacom@md2.vsnl.net.in

Madhya Pradesh

Chairman
Bp Chacko Thottumarickal
Bishop's House
Khrist Jyoti Mandir
Meghnagar – 457 779.

T: (07390) 28 48 29
F: (07390) 28 48 30
M: 094251 01047
E: chackoji@sancharnet.in

Secretary
Fr Nicholas Martis, svd
Satprakashan Sanchar Kendra
Bhanwerkua Chouraha
P. B. No.507, Indore - 452 001.

T: (0731) 23 63 733, 24 75 744
F: (0731) 247 57 31
E: nickysvd@rediffmail.com

Northern Region

Chairman
Abp Vincent M Concessao
Archbishop's House
1, Ashok Place
New Delhi – 110 001.

T: (011) 23 34 34 57, 23 34 63 75
F: (011) 23 74 65 75
E: archbish@ndf.net.in

Secretary
Fr John Paul Herman
Archbishop's House
1, Ashok Place
New Delhi – 110 001.

T: (011) 23 34 34 57, 23 36 20 58
F: (011) 23 74 65 75
M: 098682 19663
E: dr_johnpaul@hotmail.com

North East Region

Chairman
Bp Joseph Aind
Bishop of Dibrugarh
Bishop's House
P. B. No. 50, Dibrugarh - 786 001.

T: (0373) 23 24 436, 23 27 074
F: (0373) 23 21 496 (P)
E: bpjaind@hotmail.com

Secretary
Fr Peter Chinnappan
NESCOM, C/o SFS Bhavan
Sree Nagar, Dispur
Guwahati – 781 005.

T: (0361) 22 01 285
E: nescom@sancharnet.in

Orissa Region

Chairman
Bp Lucas Kerketta, sj
Bishop of Sambalpur
Bishop's House , Ainthapali
Sambalpur - 768 004.

T: (0663) 25 40 327, 25 40 295 (P)
F: (0663) 25 41 656 (O)
E: lucassmb@yahoo.co.in

Secretary
Fr Joseph Amalan, sj
St. Arnold Vikas Sanchar
P. B. No. 4
Jharsuguda – 768 201.

T: (06645) 27 34 11
F: (06645) 27 08 11
M: 094370 58411
E: aviscoms@hotmail.com

Tamil Nadu Region

Chairman
Bp Antony Devotta
Bishop of Tiruchirapalli
Bishop's House, P. B. No.14
12A Convent Road
Tiruchirapalli - 620 001.

T: (0431) 24 15 635, 24 01 014 (P)
F : (0431) 24 17 502
E: trichidio@eth.net

Secretary
Fr Vincent Chinnadurai
Santhome Comm. Centre
150, Luz Church Road
Chennai – 600 004.

T: (044) 24 67 22 18 (P)
M: 094440 28305
E: vincynam@md4.vsnl.net.in

Western Region

Chairman
Bp Godfrey de Rozari, sj
Bishop of Baroda, Bishop's House
Alkapuri - 71, Baroda - 390 007.

T: (0265) 23 11 837 (O)
F: 23 39 480 (O)
E: godfrey@wilnetonline.net

Secretary
Fr Cedric Prakash, sj
PRASHANT
P. B. 4050, Navrangpura
Ahmedabad - 380 009.

T: (079) 274 49 744, 274 55 913
F: (079) 274 89 018,
M: 098240 34536
E: sjprashant@icenet.net

11.3 Participants of the National Conference on Communications

1. Bishops

2. **Bp A.P. D'Souza**
Bishop of Mangalore
Bishop's House, Kodialbail Post
Mangalore – 575 003.
T: (0824) 24 40 524, 24 40 421 (P)
F: (0824) 24 44 035
E: bishopap@sancharnet.in

2. **Bp Agnelo Gracias**
Auxiliary Bishop of Bombay
Archbishop's House
21-Nathalal Parekh Marg
Mumbai – 400 001.
T : (022) 22 02 10 93, 22 02 1193
F : (022) 22 85 38 72
E : agnelog@rediffmail.com

3. **Bp Antony Devotta**
Bishop of Tiruchirapalli
Bishop's House, P.B. No. 14
12A Convent Road, Tiruchirapalli – 620 001.
T: (0431) 24 15 635, 24 01 014
F: (0431) 24 17 502
E : trichidio@eth.net

4. **Bp Chacko Thottumarickal**, svd
Bishop of Jhabua
Bishop's House
Meghnagar – 457 779.
T: (07390) 28 48 29
F : (07390) 28 48 30
M: 094251 01047
E: chackoji@sancharnet.in

5. **Bp Francis Kallarakal**
Bishop of Kottapuram
Bishop's House
Kottapuram - 680 667, Kerala.
T : (0480) 28 02 165, 28 02 865
F : (0480) 28 02 865
M: 098461 78921
E: kotapuram_bp@satyam.net.in

6. **Bp Godfrey de Rozario**, sj
Bishop of Baroda
Bishop's House
Alkapuri – 71
Baroda – 390 007.
T: (0265) 23 11 837
F: (0265) 23 39 480
M: 098256 87313
E : godfrey@wilnetonline.net

7. **Bp Joseph Suren Gomes**
Bishop of Krishnagar
Bishop's House
Krishnagar – 741 101.
West Bengal.
T: (03472) 25 25 54, 25 26 64 (P)
F: (03472) 25 26 64
E: bpjgomes@vsnl.net

8. **Bp Leo Cornelio**, svd
Bishop of Khandwa
Bishop's House, Khandwa – 450 001.
T: (0733) 22 22 935, 22 23 603
M: 098260 67823
E: lcornel@sancharnet.in

9. **Bp Lucas Kerketta**, svd
Bishop of Sambalpur
Bishop's House, Ainthapali
Sambalpur – 768 004.
T: (0663) 25 40 327, 25 40 295
E: lucassmb@yahoo.co.in

10. **Abp Oswald Gracias**
Archbishop of Agra
Archbishop's House
Wazirpura Road, Agra – 282 003.
T: (0562) 21 51 318, 25 26 397
M: 098370 56223
E: abpossie@sancharnet.in

11. **Bp Patrick Paul D'Souza**
Bishop of Varanasi
Bishop's House, 45-Varanasi Cantt.
Varanasi – 221 002.
T: (0542) 25 04 235, 25 00 043 (P)
M: 094152 25582
E : dovns@sify.com

12. **Bp Vincent Barwa**
Auxiliary Bishop of Ranchi
Archbishop's House, Purulia Road
P.B. 5, Ranchi - 834 001.
T: (0651) 2204728, 2201684 (P)
F: (0651) 23 04 844
M: 098101 31552
E: vincent-barwa@rediffmail.com

13. **Abp Vincent Concessao**
Archbishop of Delhi
Archbishop's House
1 Ashok Place
New Delhi - 110 001.
T: (011) 23 34 34 57, 23 36 20 58
F: (011) 23 74 65 75
E: archbish@vsnl.com

2. FABC OSC

14. **Fr Josef Franz Eilers**, svd
Executive Secretary
FABC-OSC
P. B.N. 2036, 1099 Manila.

T: (+632) 7327170
F: (+632) 7327171
E: fabc_osc@pacific.net.ph
W: www.fabc.org

3. CBCI Commission

15. **Fr Henry D'Souza**
Executive Secretary
CBCI Commission for S. Comns.
CBCI Centre, 1 Ashok Place
New Delhi - 110 001.

T: (011) 23 34 84 23, 23 34 44 70
M: 093137 82685
E: cbcimo@bol.net.in
W: www.cbcisite.com

4. Signis India

16. **Fr Dominic Emmanuel**, svd
President, Signis India
Divya Deepti Sadan
9-10 Bhai Vir Singh Marg
New Delhi - 110 001.

T: (011) 23 36 32 14, 23 36 95 82
M: 098100 18071
E: dominic1@vsnl.com

17. **Fr Peter Selvan**
Secretary, Signis India
St. Jude's Shrine
64-Cantt, Jhansi – 284 001.

T: (0542) 23 82 236, 23 83 072
M: 094154 12014
E: frpeterselvan@rediffmail.com

5. ICPA

18. **Mr Michael Gonsalves**
919 Synagogue Street
Camp, Pune - 411 001.

T: (020) 26 13 80 97, 26 13 48 57
M: 098230 84995
E: michaelgonsalves@rediffmail.com

19. **Mr K.M. Selvaraj**
Secretary, ICPA
P.O. Box 48
Ootacamund – 643 001.

T: (0423) 24 41 471
E: icpasec@yahoo.co.in

6. NISCORT

20. **Fr Sebasti L. Raj**, sj
Director, NISCORT
A-2, Sector I, Vaishali
Ghaziabad - 201 012, Uttar Pradesh.

T: (0120) 27 73 200
M: 098112 93778
E: niscort@vsnl.com

7. News Agencies

21. **Fr George Veliparambil**
Managing Director, SAR News
2/5, 4th Cross, Viveknanadnagar
M.S. Nagar, Bangalore – 560 033.

T: (080) 25 48 24 80
M : (080) 36 81 23 74
E: gvelparambil@sify.com

8. Regional Secretaries/ Directors

22. **Fr Anthony Muthu**
C/o Nav Sadhana
Tarna, Shivpur Post
Varanasi - 221 003.

T: (0542) 22 84 160, 22 83 072
E: sadhana_vns@sify.com

23. **Fr Arun Ignatius Abraham**, sj
Ravi Bharti Comns. Centre
Post Sadaquat Asharam
Patna - 800 010.

T: (0612) 26 34 55, 26 22 84
E: ravibharti@sancharnet.in

24. **Fr Cedric Prakash**, sj
Regional Secretary/ Director
P.O. Box 4050, Navrangpura
Ahmedabad - 380 009.

T: (079) 27 44 97 44, 27 45 59 13
F: (079) 27 48 90 18
M: 098240 34536
E: sjprashant@icenet.co.in

25. **Fr P. Rayappa**
Amruthavani
P.O. Box 1588, 50 Sebastian Road
Secunderabad - 500 003.

T: (040) 27 70 39 68, 27 70 11 56
F: (040) 27 70 09 57
E: amruthavani@hotmail.com

26. **Fr Denis D'Sa**
Sandesha, Premnagar
Bajjodi, Mangalore – 575 005.

T: (0824) 22 13 278, 22 25 480
M: 094480 26540
E: sandesha_d@yahoo.co.in

27. **Fr Devassy Kollamkudyil**, sdb
KCBC Media Commission
POC, Palarivattom
Kochi – 682 025.
T: (0484) 28 06 227, 28 05 815
M: (0484) 32 92 622
E: mediacom@md2.vsnl.net.in

28. **Fr John Paul Herman**, svd
Archdiocesan Media Commission
Archbishop's House
1 Ashok Place -
New Delhi-110 001.
T: (011) 23 34 34 57, 23 36 20 58
F: (011) 23 74 65 75
M: 098682 19663
E: dr_johnpaul@hotmail.com

29. **Fr Joseph Amalan**, svd
Regional Secretary/ Director
St. Arnold's Vikas Sanchar
P. B. No. 4, Jharsuguda – 768 201.
T: (06645) 27 34 11
F: (06645) 27 08 11
M: 094370 58411
E: aviscoms@hotmail.com

30. **Fr Nicholas Martis,** svd
Satprakashan Sanchar Kendra
Bhanwerkua Chouraha
P. B. No. 507, Indore – 452 001.
T: (0731) 24 75 744, 23 63 733
F: (0731) 24 75 731
E: nickysvd@rediffmail.com

31. **Fr P. J. Joseph**, sj
Chitrabani
76, Rafi Ahmed Kidwai Rd
Kolkata - 700 016.
T: (033) 22 44 01 08 (O)
F: (033) 22 45 15 07
E: cbcal@cal.vsnl.net.in

32. **Fr Vincent Chinnadurai**
Santhome Comns. Centre
Santhome, Mylapore
Chennai – 600 004.
T: (044) 24 67 22 18, 24 99 13 44
M: 098410 71321
E: vincynam@md4.vsnl.net.in

9. Editors/ Publishers

33. **Fr Alfonso Elengikal**, ssp
Editor, The Teenager
Society of St. Paul
58/23rd Road, TPS III, Bandra
Mumbai – 400 050.
T: (022) 26 40 33 12, 26 55 74 43
E: editor@theteenagermag.com

35. **Fr Charles Vas**, svd
Sangeet Natak Academy
Gyan Ashram Campus
Andheri (E), Mumbai - 400 093.
T: (022) 28 38 05 25
F: (022) 28 22 17 09
E: saa@bom7.vsnl.net.in

36. **Fr Darryl D'Souza**, sdb
Tej Prasarini
Don Bosco Communication
Matunga, Mumbai – 400 019.
T: (022) 24 15 06 80, 24 15 41 06
F: (022) 24 15 42 26
M: 098201 04342
E: tej_dbc@vsnl.net

37. **Mr Dickson Mendes**
Circulation Manager, Charisindia
National Charismatic Office
22/6, II Floor, Old Rajinder Nagar
New Delhi - 110 060.
T: (011) 25 86 42 08, 32 00 46 04
E: dickson_barbs@yahoo.co.in

38. **Fr Eric Crasta**
Editor, Raknno Weekly
Kodialbail Post
Mangalore – 575 003.
T: (0824) 24 22 426, 24 44 154
F: (0824) 24 41 904
M: 094482 54684
E: raknno@sancharnet.in

39. **Fr Francis D'Britto**
Editor, Suvarta
Giriz, Vasai – 401 201.
T: (0250) 23 26 628
M: 094226 69852
E: suvarta@vsnl.net

40. **Fr L. Anand**
Editor, Nam Vazhvu
Luz Church Road
Chennai - 600 004.
T: (044) 24 67 04 39
E: namvazhvu@vsnl.net

41. **Fr M.A. Joe Antony**, sj
Editor, The New Leader
Catholic Centre
64, Armenian Street
Chennai - 600 004.
T: (044) 25 36 23 71
F: (044) 25 38 64 22
E: nljoeant@xlweb.com

42. **Fr Sunil Rozario**
Editor, The Herald
10, Government Place East
Calcutta – 700 069.
T: (033) 24 74 869
M: 098312 75158
E: sunilrozario@vsnl.net

43. **Fr Xavier Vadakkekara,** ofm. cap.
Editor, Indian Currents
Media House
375-A, Pocket 2
Mayur Vihar Phase I
New Delhi - 110 091.

T: (011) 22 75 06 67, 22 75 13 17
M: 098103 01010
E: xavier@indiancurrents.com

10. Resource Person

44. **Mr Allwyn Fernandes**
Flat 11, PRERNA
Military Road
Marol, Andheri (E)
Mumbai – 400 059.

T: (022) 28 56 31 51
M: 09820048601
E: allwynf@vsnl.com

•••